HUMANISTIC

A Blueprint for Life

BUDDHISM

By
Venerable Master Hsing Yun

Translated by
John Balcom, Ph.D.

© 2003 Buddha's Light Publishing (First Edition)
© 2005 Buddha's Light Publishing (Revised Edition)

By Venerable Master Hsing Yun
Translated by John Balcom, Ph.D
Edited by Robin Stevens and Edmond Chang
Book designed by Ching Tay and Dung Trieu
Cover designed by Mei-Chi Shih

Published by Buddha's Light Publishing
3456 South Glenmark Drive
Hacienda Heights, CA 91745

ISBN 1-932293-03-5

CONTENTS

Foreword

Buddhism is often perceived as a religion that places an emphasis on the dark side of life: on death, dying, and suffering. Due to this perception, it is little wonder that the charge of pessimism has been leveled against it, perhaps more frequently than any other religion. It is a charge that often obliges apologists and scholars to provide cautionary statements disputing this viewpoint. Yet, it must be said that there is a modicum of truth to this perception, although not to the extent of reducing Buddhism to a one-dimensional stereotype. It is true that this attitude comes in part from within the Buddhist community, which often identifies Buddhist practice with funerals, and Buddhist inquiry with the world beyond: the world of ghosts and demons. Is it any wonder, then, that Buddhism might be viewed as an impractical religion vis-à-vis the solution to life's problems? Furthermore, the pursuit of the "other-worldly" is fine for the scholar and religious professional, but does it meet the needs of the "man on the street?" More pressing to the latter are issues that affect the lives in the here and now, issues of right and wrong in all its manifestations. Certainly Buddhists are aware of the five virtues so prominently proclaimed in Buddhism and recognized and accepted as the basis of living the Buddhist life. To know these five, however, only in the most general and superficial manner and not to consider all the real-life issues that arise from following one or more of these virtues, especially taking a life or stealing, is not very helpful to individuals who need to understand the consequences of avoiding or pursuing certain actions in the context of present-day circumstances.

The myriad issues that arise in the pursuit of living good and decent lives cannot be ignored. Buddhist teaching provides the foundation for judging what is right and wrong, proper and improper, beneficial and malevolent, but the decision cannot be based solely on theoretical and doctrinal pronouncements. Judgments must be reached through careful deliberations taking into account all of the consequences of the action.

The move to a more practical, "this-worldly" Buddhism has been an on-going phenomenon over a number of decades. One of the early expressions of this more practical form of Buddhism in China was introduced by Venerable T'ai Hsu (Taixu: 1889~1947), the monastic who introduced the term "Humanistic Buddhism," a form of Buddhism that was designed to transform society and bring about human progress.

Humanistic Buddhism is also the label used to describe the Fo Guang Shan Buddhist Order and monastery in Kaohsiung, Taiwan, and the 200 plus temples and monasteries throughout the world. Despite the impression that Humanistic Buddhism is a recent innovation, the founder of the Fo Guang Shan Buddhist Order, Grand Master Hsing Yun has stressed on numerous occasions that it is not a later version of Buddhism, but rather, in the words of the Grand Master, "the Buddhism of the Buddha himself." Furthermore, this Buddhism of the Buddha is understood to be the Mahayana tradition, specifically the Bodhisattva path. This is what is meant by "practical Dharma."

Very often, the "scriptures" of Buddhism leave the impression that the Buddha and his community were *only* interested in issues within the monastic community, on specific points of doctrine, and on the ultimate goal of Nirvana. What is stressed here is the term "only," for there were other matters of concern: issues in politics, economics, and in pursuing the good life within the lay community, issues that were not exclusively associated with the Buddha's teaching but could nonetheless be illuminated by this teaching. This renewed awareness that Buddhism is not only reserved for the elite but for all humans reflects Master Hsing Yun's ongoing commitment that the Buddha's teaching is "humanistic"–humanistic because the Buddha was human and because all his teachings are there, but one need not assume nor achieve a special status to be transformed. It is revealing that Master Hsing Yun looks to Masters Taixu and Huineng as his predecessors and that both come from a tradition that finds no difference between the cycle of ignorant existence (samsara) and that of complete freedom from this cycle (nirvana). Liberation and transformation do not come about only after this life but might even be attained in this very life: an attainment for all, not only for "saints" but also for sinners.

Venerable Master Hsing Yun has provided a valuable service to all Buddhists because he has reminded Buddhists that the true message of the Dharma is the practice of love, compassion, wisdom, and all the virtues that lead to these qualities.

The present book, *Humanistic Buddhism: A Blueprint for Life*, is the clearest exposition yet of Humanistic Buddhism. It is Buddhism minus the regional, doctrinal, ritual, and traditional limitations that so often equate Buddhism with a particular ethnic or cultural group. It is a Buddhism that seeks to improve the individual and society, the inner self and the outer social environment. It discusses the physical body, emotions, morality and ethics, relationships with family and society, government, globalism, and nature and the environment: in brief, the human condition in its entirety. The lessons readers take from this book are the responsibility of the reader; but there can be no doubt that this book is a storehouse of wisdom that is readily accessible by one and all.

James A. Santucci
Department of Comparative Religion
California State University
Fullerton, CA 92834-6868

Preface

Since its inception, Humanistic Buddhism has become widely established, spreading its roots throughout China, Taiwan, and many other places in the world. In Japan, the thought and practice of Humanistic Buddhism is widespread, even though the term "Humanistic Buddhism" is not used. For example, Japanese temples are open to the public, monastics work in society, and a patronage system is in place. Buddhist communities in Japan have also founded universities and opened department stores. In Korea, Buddhist groups with long histories have gradually modernized and even established television stations. All of these events are indications that Humanistic Buddhism is the wave of the future.

In addition to these trends, Mahayana Buddhism is already practiced in Vietnam, Malaysia, Indonesia, and the Philippines. Humanistic Buddhism is the bodhisattva path of Mahayana Buddhism. In some areas where the Theravada School is practiced, Hinayana Buddhism and the original form of Buddhism are still practiced as well. However, more recently, people with a vision for the future development of Buddhism in Sri Lanka, Thailand, and Myanmar have been leaning toward Humanistic Buddhism. For example, the Dharmakaya Temple in Thailand enjoys massive popular support; from the name of the temple, we can see that Thai Buddhists are actively on the way to the bodhisattva path.

On February 6, 2001, Dhammananda, a nun from Thailand, publicly received the sramanera precepts at the Tapodaramaya Temple in Sri Lanka, thereby challenging long-standing traditions. Venerable Tep Vong of the Mahasangha School in Kampuchea; Venerable Pandith Talalle Dharmaloka Anunayaka Thera, the most senior monk of western Sri Lanka; Kumburugamawe Vajira Maha Thera, vice president of the Buddhist Pali University of Sri Lanka; Dr. Mapalagama Wipulasara Maha Thera, director of the Maha Bodhi Society of India; Bhiksu Ashwaghosh, editor-in-chief of the Dharmmakirti (Buddhist Monthly) in Nepal; Phra Maha Somchai Prohmsuwan, vice president of the Maha Chula Buddhist University in Thailand; and other virtuous and eminent monks joined together and attended the ceremony for transmitting the sramanera and sramanerika precepts, the bhiksu and bhiksuni precepts, and the bodhisattva precepts in India and undertook the task of serving as witnesses for ordinations. The International Buddhist Progress Society in Sri Lanka has published books on Humanistic Buddhism and also held a publication reception at Tapodarmaya Temple in Colombo, which was attended by more than three hundred monastics and devotees, including the likes of Venerable A. Sn Rahula, chairman of the Lohana group; the Vinaya scholar K. Nandaratana; Professor Daya Edirisinghe of the Philosophy Department of Kelaniya University; and Senarat Wijayasundara, vice chairman of the Sri Lanka Buddhist Association.

These examples demonstrate that the trumpet of Humanistic Buddhism has sounded and has been heard in all corners of the globe and is, undoubtedly, widely known. Humanistic Buddhism is not limited to a region or a people. It derives directly from the teachings of the Buddha; it is the religion of the Dharma bequeathed by the Buddha. Humanistic Buddhism is concerned with the enlightenment of humanity. If an individual or a group desires to be accepted, they must contribute politically or economically to society. By the same token, Buddhism will have value only to the extent to which it can meet the needs of the times, providing people with joy and happiness. Otherwise it will die out.

Buddhism is rich in resources, including literature, art, and music, all of which can be causes for the liberation of sentient beings. However, in the past, such resources were insufficiently utilized. Instead, Buddhism had emphasized an awareness of impermanence, non-self, suffering, and emptiness. It had never been humanistic or constructive, and for this reason had never flourished until now.

Over the last sixty years, I have promoted a Humanistic Buddhism that is part and parcel of life, not separate from it. Humanistic Buddhism is not the creation of Fo Guang Shan. The rationale for Humanistic Buddhism derives from the Buddha, the founder of Buddhism, because the Buddha was born, cultivated the path, became enlightened, and strived to enlighten others in this mortal world. For the Buddha, it is this world that should take precedence. He lived among the people, and what he transmitted is Humanistic Buddhism.

Humanistic Buddhism is the Buddhism needed in our daily lives. In the past, Buddhism placed more emphasis on leaving the world and living apart from it in the forests and mountains. Today, Buddhism is forsaking the forests and mountains for society, spreading from the temples to homes. Buddhism is living life, making life happier and family life more joyful, and adding harmony to human relations, the mind, and the spirit. The following gatha is the Buddha's Light International Association members' maxim:

> *May kindness, compassion, joy, and equanimity*
> *pervade all dharma realms.*
> *May all beings benefit from our blessings and friendship.*
> *May our ethical practice of Chan and Pure Land*
> *help us to realize equality and patience.*
> *May we undertake the Great Vows with humility and gratitude.*

This gatha illustrates the bodhisattva way of Humanistic Buddhism. It is based on humanity with the family as its core. It possesses the non-discriminating universality of Avalokitesvara, who with great compassion and loving-kindness, selflessly helps all beings, putting the Dharma into practice in this world. Humanistic Buddhism encompasses all these ideals.

Humanistic Buddhism stresses the purification of life through ethical thought, and the elevation of both mind and spirit. If you believe in the Law of Cause and Effect and practice it in your life, then the Law of Cause and Effect is Humanistic Buddhism. If you believe in compassion and practice it in your life, then compassion is Humanistic Buddhism. Taking refuge in the Triple Gem, the five precepts, the six perfections, and the ten wholesome conducts all are Humanistic Buddhism. Humanistic Buddhism is Buddhism that seeks to liberate all sentient beings.

Without exception, all of the following constitute Humanistic Buddhism: writing books and developing theories; establishing and running schools; building temples and Dharma centers; discussing Chan over vegetarian meals; lecturing on the sutras and expounding the Dharma; cleaning streets and protecting the environment; engaging in educational and cultural activities; providing free medical care; caring for the elderly and educating the young; practicing the Dharma and transmitting the precepts; giving lectures on Buddhism; making pilgrimages to temples; reciting the Buddhas' names and practicing Dharma with others; giving Buddhist examinations; singing Buddhist songs and chanting sutras; teaching the Dharma to the troops; carrying the teachings to the countryside; and nurturing wisdom and skill. Upholding the precepts in life constitutes Humanistic Buddhism. The relationship between oneself and others based on dependent origination is Humanistic Buddhism, as is the cyclical Law of Cause and Effect, the karma of good and bad, the successful extinction of suffering and the attainment of peace in this life, the world embracing everything with its nature of emptiness, and true self-fulfillment.

Humanistic Buddhism places more weight on reality than abstract discussion, on all sentient beings rather than the individual, on society rather than temples in the mountains and forests, and on benefiting others more than oneself. Humanistic Buddhism is any doctrine that increases happiness in life.

The purpose of this book is not to discuss the theory of Humanistic Buddhism, nor to adhere to the conventions of a scholarly work, although it regrets the sometimes hair-splitting, theoretical debates and divisive ideas of some past scholars that unfortunately once split Buddhism apart. Actually, from the very beginning, Buddhism has been "only one vehicle, not two or three." In fact, its rationale as one that stems from a single faith is not in dispute. This also applies to the reading of the sutras. Their meaning is clear, but once we read the commentaries, we are often confused by the varied interpretations. The intention of scholarly Buddhist writing should be to provide people with confidence, understanding, consistency, and mastery through comprehensive study. For example, prajna-wisdom is often mentioned in Buddhism for the purpose of erasing distinctions. However, in the past, various schools and sects of Buddhism have argued about it again and again, until they each had a different interpretation for the same concept. Although it is said that Buddhism is vast and profound, all the various misinterpreted commentaries have not helped Buddhist practitioners to cultivate and attain enlightenment. Clearly, we do not like to argue about the Dharma. What we need is the single vehicle of Humanistic Buddhism to help us get to the heart of the matter.

Humanistic Buddhism may be easy to understand, but in reality it is difficult to practice. In Buddhist circles today, there is no end to the teaching and discussion of the scriptures. Yet it is difficult to expound on Humanistic Buddhism. Even if one can talk about it, it tends to be superficial and very difficult to put into practice. Humanistic Buddhism is the practical Dharma. In which aspect of life–walking, dwelling, sitting, lying down, eating, dressing, or thinking–can we depart from Humanistic Buddhism?

In order to help people understand Humanistic Buddhism more thoroughly, in this book I will briefly discuss each of the following topics, drawing from experiences described in the Buddhist scriptures and examples of virtuous behavior from the past:

1. Ethics–the way of home life
2. Morality–the way of cultivation
3. Livelihood–the way of using resources
4. Emotions–the way of love and affection
5. Society–the way of oneself and others
6. Loyalty and Filial Piety–the way of establishing oneself
7. Wealth–the way of financial management
8. Long life and happiness–the way of ownership

9. Maintaining good health–the way of medicine
10. Loving-kindness and Compassion–the way of affinity
11. Cause and effect–the way of dependent origination
12. Religion–the way of faith
13. Life–the way of birth and death
14. Knowledge–the way of study
15. Education and amusement–the way of correct life
16. Rituals–the way of right views
17. Nature–the way of environmental protection
18. Government–the way of participating in politics
19. International affairs–the way of tolerance
20. The future–the way of development

It is my sincere hope that through these teachings I can help to pro-vide a blueprint for life and articulate the ideals of Humanistic Buddhism for all.

Acknowledgments

We received a lot of help from many people and we want to thank them for their efforts in making the publication of this book possible. We especially appreciate Venerable Tzu Jung, the Chief Executive of the Fo Guang Shan International Translation Center (F.G.S.I.T.C.), Venerable Hui Chi, Abbot of Hsi Lai Temple; Venerable Yi Chao and Venerable Miao Hsi for their support and leadership; John Balcom, Ph.D., for his translation; Robin Stevens and Edmond Chang for their editing; Venerable Man Jen, Mu-Tzen Hsu, Pey-Rong Lee, and Kevin Hsyeh for proofreading and preparing the manuscript for publication; Mei-Chi Shih for book cover design; and Ching Tay and Dung Trieu for their book design. Our appreciation also goes to everyone who has supported this project from its conception to its completion.

HUMANISTIC

A Blueprint for Life

BUDDHISM

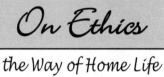

On Ethics

the Way of Home Life

Ethics serves an important function in the harmonizing of human relations. In a family there are close relationships between father and mother, brothers and sisters, uncles and aunts, husband and wife, brothers- and sisters-in-law, among others. However, order and harmony in a family can only be guaranteed by maintaining hierarchical ethical relationships based on love and respect between young and old. As part of its Chinese Cultural Revival Movement, the Republic of China government promoted science, democracy, and ethics. Clearly, ethics is an important part of Chinese culture.

Ever since Buddhism first entered China during the Eastern Han Dynasty[1] period, primacy has always been given to the monks and nuns living in monasteries. For this reason, most people assume that Buddhism emphasizes renouncing worldly life and becoming a monastic and is rarely concerned with family life. In fact, Buddhism is made up of four groups–bhiksus, bhiksunis, upasikas, and upasakas–and it stresses the value of ethics. For example, the *Sutra of the Buddha of Infinite Life* [*Sukhavativyuha Sutra*] tells us that family members "should treat one another with love and respect and not hatred and jealousy." With regard to daily necessities, "family members should share things with each other and not be greedy." In our daily lives together, we should "be tender in word and look and not be disagreeable with each other." From the words of this sutra, we clearly see that the Buddha's teachings are deeply and concretely imbued with humanistic character and the strength of life.

The family is at the center of every person's life. Human ethics begin with filial piety, which is the practical basis of ethics and morality. For this reason, Buddhism advocates filial piety as the first and foremost of all human relationships. Buddhism holds that filial devotion to one's parents and repaying parental kindness is one of the four great kindnesses to one's elders. The opposite is patricide and matricide, both of which are among the five great violations. The *Sutra on Contemplation of the Buddha of Infinite Life* [*Amitayurdhyana Sutra*] sees filial devotion as an important basis for being reborn in the Pure Land.

In the past, the Confucian path of filial devotion emphasized caring for one's parents during their lifetime and burying them with the proper rites upon death; greeting one's parents in the morning and at night; maintaining a pleasant countenance; and being respectful and harmonious. Buddhism also holds that a person should "do one's utmost in one's entire life to care for one's parents, and not to do so is a grave crime" (*Five Part Vinaya* [*Mahisasaka Vinaya*]). The *Connected Discourses of the Buddha* [*Samyuktagama Sutra*] states: "Care for your parents and elders amiably and with respectful words; set aside coarse words and avoid being double-tongued." Buddhism goes a step further and teaches that "food, drink, and even treasure are not sufficient to repay the kindness of one's parents; leading them to know and believe the right Dharma[2] is the only way to fully repay one's parents for their kindness" (*Sutra Discoursed by the Inconceivable Light Bodhisattva* [*Busiyi Guang Pusa Suoshuo Jing*]).

In his *Record of Monastics' Virtuous Deeds* [*Zimen Chongxing Lu*], Master Lianchi[3] divides filial piety into three levels. He refers to "caring for one's parents during their lifetime and burying them with the proper rites upon death" as lesser filial piety; "honoring one's parents and ancestors" as moderate filial piety; and "leading one's parents from the cycle of birth and death" as the greatest filial piety. For this reason, both the *Jataka Sutras* and the *Sutra of the Filial Child Discoursed by the Buddha* [*Fo Shuo Xiaozi Jing*] uniformly assert, "converting one's parents is the truest way to repay parental kindness." In other words, "if one's parents do not believe, then awaken their faith; if one's parents are not upholding the precepts, then lead them to dwell with the prohibitions; if one's parents are by nature stingy and closed-minded, then awaken in them wisdom. If a child can do this, then that is the first step toward repaying parental kindness" (*Vinaya*).

Buddhist filial piety transcends ordinary filial piety. In the past, most people believed that "from our parents we receive our bodies and they are not to be harmed." From this traditional perspective, then, for a monastic to shave his/her head and renounce the world and love and bid farewell to his/her parents is very unfilial behavior. Throughout the Buddhist scriptures, however, there are examples of people who strove to become models of filial piety. The Buddha "carried his father's coffin" (*Sutra on the Nirvana of King Suddhodana Discoursed by the Buddha [Fo Shuo Jingfan Wang Boniepan Jing]*), and "spoke the Dharma to his mother" (*Sutra on the Buddha's Ascension to the Trayastrimsas Heaven to Discourse the Dharma to His Mother [Fo Sheng Daoli Tian Wei Mu Shuofa Jing]*). The *Sutra of Wisdom and Foolishness [Xian Yu Jing]* and the *Syamaka Sutra [Shanzi Jing]* both recognize that "the Buddha was honored in three realms for his benevolence and filial piety."

There are many other examples. The honored Maudgalyayana sought to free his mother from the sufferings of the realm of hell (*Ullumbana Sutra [Yulanpan Jing]*); before entering parinirvana, Sariputra made a special trip home to say good-bye to his mother and repay her kindness (*Sutra of Wisdom and Foolishness [Damamuka-nidana Sutra]*); during the Ming Dynasty,[4] Venerable Master Ouyi[5] sought to prolong the life of his ill mother with sincere prayers (*Biography of Venerable Master Ouyi [Ouyi Dashi Zhuan]*); and during the Period of the Republic of China,[6] the monk Xuyun worshipped for three years at Mt. Wutai[7] to repay his mother's kindness (*Chronicle of Master Xuyun [Xuyun Heshang Nianpu]*). Then there are the examples of Daoming,[8] who wove mats for his mother; Shibei,[9] who achieved the Way to repay his father; Daopi,[10] who demonstrated sincerity by gathering his father's scattered bones; and Zongying, who recited the Buddha's name to save his mother (*Record of Monastics' Virtuous Deeds [Zimen Chongxing Lu]*). All these examples demonstrate that although those who have left home may live by a different set of relationships, they have not forsaken the filial duty of caring for their parents. As a result, many stories of moving deeds have been passed down to us. For example, there is the story of novice[11] Huixin's mother, who encouraged him to work hard and strive for Buddhahood and not for the glory bestowed by the emperor. There is the story of Dongshan Liangjie,[12] who in his *Letter of Farewell to My Mother*, indicated his resolve to seek the Way. Although his mother wept day and night, she put aside her love for her son and sent him a reply, encouraging him to cultivate himself so that he might achieve enlightenment.

In promoting filial devotion, Buddhism not only promotes "filial piety," "making offerings to monastics," and "respecting the practice of purification" as its teachings (*Great Compilation of Monastic Rules* [*Mahasangha Vinaya*]), it goes even further by stressing the importance of such deeds. The *Sutra on the Contemplation of the Mind* [*Xindi Guan Jing*] declares: "The blessings accrued from caring for one's parents are the same as those from making offerings to the Buddha. Filial respect should always be on one's mind." The *Sutra on the Difficulty of Repaying the Kindness of Parents* [*Fumu Enzhong Nanbao Jing*] holds: "Even if one were to carry one's father on the left shoulder and one's mother on the right shoulder, so that one's skin was pressed to the bone and through the bone to the marrow, around Mt. Sumeru for countless kalpas, until one's blood flowed and one's ankles gave way, it would still be insufficient to repay the kindness of one's parents." These examples are a clear indication of how important filial piety is in Buddhism.

In society, laypeople have their own set of relationships; in Buddhism, monastics have master-disciple relationships and relationships between Dharma brothers and sisters. The *Four Part Vinaya* [*Dharmagupta Vinaya*] says, "A master looks upon his/her followers as if they were sons and daughters; and the followers look upon their master as if he/she were a father or mother. And when they respect one another, the right Dharma will be held longer." According to the *Imperially Reviewed Encyclopedia of the Taiping Era* [*Taiping Yulan*], "The teacher is the basis of a student's learning; the student who has a teacher can be compared to a tree with roots." The *Sutra of Loyalty* [*Zhong Xin Jing*] states, "After achieving the Way, one appreciates the kindness of a teacher."

At times, the relationship between a Buddhist master and disciple is deeper than that of kinship. For example, during the Jin Dynasty,[13] Tanyin fell dangerously ill. His disciple, Fakuang,[14] repented for his master with great devotion for seven days and seven nights (*Records of Monastics at Tianmu Mountain* [*Xi Tianmu Zushan Zhi*]). In the Yuan Dynasty,[15] even when Yinjian[16] met with the hardships of war, he continued to serve his master, Zhong'guan Zhaogong, with the same devotion, earning him the respect of the Yuan troops (*History of the Buddhist Patriarchs* [*Fozu Lidai Tongzai*]). Bumao waited on Chan Master Niaoke[17] for sixteen years before he was given instruction and finally realized his true nature (*Jingde Records of the Transmission of the Lamp* [*Jingde Chuan Deng Lu*]). In the Song Dynasty,[18] Huaizhi reverently obeyed the last wishes of Zhenjing Kewen,[19] his teacher, steadfastly refusing to become the abbot of the temple and to lead others, forfeiting fame and fortune (*Compendium of the Five Records of Chan Teaching* [*Wu Deng Huiyuan*]).

In addition, there are instances that illustrate the mutual benefits of teaching and learning between master and student, where both became persons of exemplary virtue. There is the example of Venerable Daozhen, who steadfastly followed the orders of his disciple who served as abbot. He poured tea and prepared fruit for guests, enjoying the bitter as if it were the sweet. If we could learn from the spirit of Daozhen and his willingness to reverse roles, we might be able to eliminate many of the problems we experience today that are associated with generational gaps.

Everything exists because of the coming together of causes and conditions. The accumulation of causes and conditions leads to existence, and with the extinguishing of causes and conditions, things pass away. Even if the relationship is as close as that of parents and children, when the conditions end, separation is inevitable. Therefore, people should always cherish their time together and help each other. The *Sutra on the Contemplation of the Mind* says, "When one's compassionate mother is at home, it is as if one possesses wealth; and when she is away, it is as if one is impoverished. When the compassionate mother is alive, it is like sunrise; and when she passes away, it is like sunset." The most blessed circumstance in this world is while one's parents are both alive. Therefore, children should always care for their parents while they are still living.

People should show filial obedience to their parents. How can one be a human being and not show filial obedience? In addition to frequently emphasizing and explaining filial piety, such as in the statement, "The kindness of a loving father is as great as a mountain; the kindness of a merciful mother is as deep as the sea" (*Sutra on the Contemplation of the Mind*), the Buddhist sutras go a step further in wanting us to "see all people as Buddhas, and think of all sentient beings as parents" (*Sutra of Contemplation on the Practicing Methods of Samantabhadra Bodhisattva* [*Guan Puxian Pusa Xing Fa Jing*]). The idea that "every man is like my father; every woman, like my mother" (*Brahma Net Sutra* [*Fanwang Jing*]) expands the scope of the family to include all sentient beings.

Ordinary people such as ourselves are not able to see all sentient beings as our father, our mother, or even as Buddhas. On household relationships such as between parents and children, husband and wife, relatives, employers and employees, and even between master and disciple, the *Long Discourses of the Buddha* [*Dirghagama Sutra*] states:

> Children should show respect for their parents in five ways, by: 1) supporting and attending to them, and making sure their needs are satisfied, 2) first notifying their parents when they want to do something, 3) obeying the wishes of their parents, 4) not rebelling against the authority of their parents, and 5) continuing and enhancing their parents' profession.
>
> Parents, too, should raise and educate their children by: 1) teaching their children not to do anything destructive, 2) instructing and guiding them in good ways, 3) deeply loving and looking after them, 4) properly arranging good marriages for them, and 5) providing them with an appropriate allowance.
>
> A husband should show respect for his wife by: 1) treating her with respect and love, 2) being dignified and decent, 3) aptly providing daily necessities, 4) being serious when appropriate, and 5) entrusting her with household matters.
>
> A wife should show respect for her husband by: 1) showing

him consideration, respect, and love, 2) being neat and tidy, 3) being warm and affectionate, 4) being sincere and honest, and 5) praising and complimenting him.

A person should show respect for his or her relatives by: 1) giving charity, 2) saying kind words, 3) benefiting others, 4) sharing things, and 5) not taking advantage of others.

Relatives should show respect for one of their own by: 1) guiding the wild and unrestrained, 2) protecting those who lose wealth because of their unrestrained ways, 3) protecting the fearful, 4) not admonishing each other in public, and 5) praising each other.

An employer should show respect for his/her employees by: 1) applying himself when able, 2) supplying food and drink appropriately, 3) working as the occasion demands, 4) giving medical treatment when ill, and 5) allowing time for rest.

An employee should show respect for his/her employer by: 1) rising early, 2) doing a thorough job, 3) not taking what is not given, 4) doing his/her work correctly and effectively, and 5) supporting and praising his/her employer appropriately.

A disciple should show respect for his/her teacher by: 1) attending to him/her properly, 2) making offerings and respecting him/her, 3) looking up to him/her, 4) following his/her instructions, and 5) upholding the Dharma from the teacher and never forgetting it.

A teacher should show respect for his/her disciple by: 1) teaching according to his disciples' ability to learn the Dharma, 2) instructing the disciple in what he/she has never heard, 3) explaining and answering his/her questions, 4) showing his friendliness and kindness, and 5) not being sparing in instruction.

The Confucians used to say: "The aged will be cared for to the end, the mature will work, the young will be nurtured, and widowers, widows, the unmarried, and the handicapped will all be cared for." For the layperson observing today's Humanistic Buddhism, wisdom should be used in handling the emotions surrounding human relations. The Dharma is used to purify, beautify, spread, and add Buddhism to lay life. The aged, middle-aged, and the young should treat one another with love and respect, kindness, and filial piety, as well as teach and advise one another, because familial relations are interlinked. Fathers, mothers, sons, and daughters are all held together like inseparable links in a chain. Each person must do his or her utmost to love and respect others and strive for harmony. For only when a family laughs together will familial relations be happy and harmonious.

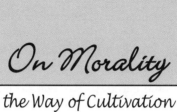

On Morality

the Way of Cultivation

Morality is something that should be cultivated, as it is the one thing that sets humans apart from animals. Morality is what ensures that there will be law and order in a nation. If the people of a nation lose their moral standards, then government officials will be corrupt, using public office for private gain; businesspeople will steal and deceive; doubt and jealousy will arise among friends, leading to harm and slander; there will be discord, deception, and lying between neighbors; and society will be rife with foolishness and fallacy. Everywhere people will struggle with one another for their own benefit, profiting at the expense of others with no sense of shame. Thus, it is only by cultivating a sense of morality and by leading a moral life that society will be harmonious, families will be happy, friends will keep promises, and we will be able to help one another.

What we generally refer to as morality is the conscious attempt to benefit society. By contrast, immorality is to infringe upon others and to undermine social order. Buddhism is a religion that places humanity at the center of everything, and Buddhist moral standards are reason, law, and guidance. For example, according to the *Dharma Garden of Buddhism* [*Fayuan Zhulin*], "Entering the court, one assists the king with determination and loyalty; at home one assists one's parents with respect, sincerity, filial piety, and loyalty." It continues, "If one yearns and strives for good, one will be able to settle down; if one yearns for and strives to be filial and respectful, one will honor one's parents."

In the *Collection of Great Treasures* [*Da Bao Ji Jing*], we are advised, "Do not lead others astray; reconcile with those who cannot get along with others; study adequately; and avoid double-tongued people." According to the *Sutra on the Buddha of Infinite Life*, "Coarse language harms oneself and others–it is harmful to all. Cultivating and using good language benefits oneself and others–it is mutually beneficial." The *Sutra of Illuminating Light* [*Chu Yao Jing*] states, "Those who harm others will themselves be harmed; those who complain about others will themselves be complained about; those who curse others will themselves be cursed; those who attack others will themselves be attacked." The *Surata Sutra Discoursed by the Buddha* [*Suratapariprccha Sutra*] also asserts, "Deception is the root of all unwholesomeness. Cutting off wholesome deeds results in the accumulation of suffering. How does it profit a person to lie?" Morality, then, is our path of cultivation.

In Buddhism, the five precepts and ten wholesome conducts set the standards for human morality. They encourage us to commit no wrong-doings and only practice good deeds, and not to infringe on the body, wealth, reputation, or dignity of others. They can completely transform the human heart and provide order to the network of human relations for the improvement of society. For Buddhists, practicing the six perfections is the criterion for a moral life. Of the six perfections, upholding the precepts, meditation, and prajna-wisdom are considered the "three studies." They can cure the three poisons–greed, anger, and ignorance–and restrain human selfishness. If a person upholds the precepts, he or she will not be selfish; without selfishness, greed will not arise. By meditating, a person will not harm others; without harm, anger will not arise. If a person cultivates prajna-wisdom, he/she will not be ignorant; without ignorance, stupidity cannot exist. Once greed, anger, and ignorance are eliminated and a person practices charitable behavior, then a benevolent and compassionate heart will manifest itself naturally. By practicing patience, it will be possible for a person to perfect a resolute spirit. By practicing diligence, a person will be filled with a fearless strength.

Therefore, the five precepts of Buddhism should be considered the foundation of morality to be observed by everyone. The ten wholesome conducts constitute an enlarged and improved morality for purifying the human heart and elevating human character. Cause and effect and karmic retribution are the unchanging morality of good and bad in this world. The six perfections are the moral basis of the Mahayana bodhisattva practice of benefiting and enlightening oneself and others.

According to the *Book of Rites* [*Da Dai Liji*],[20] "One who has achieved the Way understands what is moral; those who are moral therefore respect the Way. That is why the immoral is not respected and that which is not the Way is incomprehensible." Zhou Dunyi[21] says, "Correct action is the Way, and its harmonious use is called morality." He goes on to assert, "In all of heaven and earth, that which is most respected is the Way, and that which is most valued is morality." Buddhism and Confucianism are alike in that they both emphasize a moral life. Confucius never spoke of strange phenomenon or spirits; and true Buddhism never praises extraordinary beings or the occult, but rather places emphasis on compassionate morality.

Observing the four means of embracing and the six perfections; adhering to the five precepts and ten wholesome conducts; upholding right understanding and views; giving charity and forming good affinities; not bearing old grudges; demonstrating repentance and gratitude; protecting the six sense organs;[22] blessing and giving joy to the living; repaying the four kindnesses; widely sharing the Dharma for the benefit of all sentient beings; showing respectfulness and forgiveness; maintaining kindheartedness and loving words of praise; protecting right mindfulness; being selfless in sacrificing oneself and working for others. These are all examples of moral behavior espoused by Buddhism.

According to the *Precious Teachings of the Chan Masters* [*Chanlin Baoxun*], Chan Master Mingjiao Qisong[23] of the Song Dynasty once made the following analogy: If a person were to be compared to the tyrants Jie, Zhou, Li, and You,[24] he or she would be angry; but if the same person were compared to Boyi or Shuqi,[25] then he or she would be happy. Jie and Zhou, harsh as they were, were still the people's kings. On the contrary, Boyi and Shuqi were paupers. Why would one be happy about this comparison and not the other? The answer lies in the difference between having and not having morality. This same philosophy is reflected in the following statement from the *Collective Sutra on Six Perfections* [*Liu Du Ji Jing*]: "I'd rather hew to the Way and die in poverty than be born with wealth and never do anything moral."

Song Dynasty Chan Master Fenyang Wude[26] also observed, "Today, knowledge is emphasized; in ancient times, morality was emphasized. They mutually reinforce one another and appropriately guide us." In this world, everyone has the responsibility to transform society through just guidance. Those who are virtuous can always influence others through moral example.

Most people think that possessing wealth gives life value and that having rank gives life meaning. However, the true meaning of life has little to do with any of this. A moral life is what is most important and meaningful. There are many examples of individuals who emphasized moral cultivation in the Buddhist scriptures. The following are just a few:

> One should love those who are virtuous and take delight when others perform wholesome acts. One should never be envious (*Sutra on the Auspicious and Inauspicious Conducts Requested by Ananda* [*Anan Wen Shi Fo Ji Xiong Jing*]).
>
> Praise a person's good deeds; do not point out a person's faults; speak not of that which brings a person shame. Listen to a person's secrets, but tell no one else (*Sutra on Upasaka Precepts* [*Upasakasila Sutra*]).
>
> Do not talk about another's faults and do not point out the wrongdoings of another. Avoid coarse language and stinginess (*Collection of Great Treasures*).
>
> Cultivate oneself without examining the good or bad of others and judge not others with word or thought; then one's karmas of body, speech, and mind will be purified (*Historical Records of the Dharma Gem* [*Lidai Fabao Ji*]).
>
> Witnessing the shortcomings of others, one should remain silent, but one should always acknowledge one's own limitations (*Important Selections from the Sutras* [*Zhu Jing Yao Ji*]).

Always reflect on one's own mistakes, but do not remind others of their own shortcomings (*Vimalakirti Sutra* [*Vimalakirtintirdesa Sutra*]).

Seeing others commit good deeds, one should exert the same efforts; encountering limitations, one should not imitate them at all costs. One should always behave as if one is receiving an honored guest (*Vigilance for All Monastics* [*Zimen Jingxun*]).

Constantly review your own behavior, but do not look at the shortcomings of others. Be harmonious and do not contend with others (*Moon Lamp Samadhi Sutra* [*Samadhiraja-chadrapradipa Sutra*]).

Always speak kind words; avoid negative or destructive speech (*Sutra of the Ten Great Dharma Wheels* [*Dasacakra-ksitigarbha Sutra*]).

Do not look for the shortcomings of others; do not discriminate against others; do not be covetous of others' possessions; forsake all negative words (*Sutra on the Mindfulness and Purification of the Mind* [*Fajue Jingxin Jing*]).

Seeing the world's ills, comfort oneself according to the Dharma (*Five Part Vinaya*).

Turn the other cheek to blows and curses; do not return hate for hate; maintain a calm mind with angry people; and do not imitate other people's wrongdoings (*Repentance Text of the Mahisasaka School* [*Mishase Jiemo Ben*]).

In times of happiness, do not treat others lightly; seeing others suffer, one should not be happy (*Sutra on Upasaka Precepts*).

Confucius reasoned, "The virtue of a gentleman is like the wind; that of a small man like the grass. The grass must bow before the wind." If one influences others by one's own virtuous behavior, others will gladly follow suit. Therefore, if we wish to have a respectable career and life overall, it is of the utmost importance to cultivate virtue and lead a virtuous life.

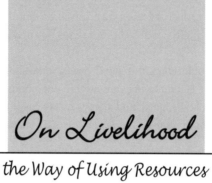

On Livelihood

the Way of Using Resources

Everyone must live his or her own day-to-day life. Although food, clothing, shelter, and transportation are the basic necessities of life, everyone has different demands when it comes to material things–some only want to eat exotic delicacies, live in luxury high rises, wear silks and satins, and drive luxury cars; whereas, others feel coarse tea, plain food, and homemade things are sufficient for a happy, carefree life. Therefore, no objective material standard for a happy life exists–everyone is different.

Buddhism does not demand asceticism from all believers where daily life is concerned. Regarding food, one should eat one's fill; regarding clothing, one should dress appropriately. However, no one should use resources wastefully. Materialism can easily awaken our desires, giving rise to greed. Material things can be exhausted, but desire is endless. Once seduced by materialism, suffering will only increase. For this reason, followers of Buddhism tend to opt for a simple life with few material possessions. Traveling monastics can roam the world over with nothing but "three robes and an alms bowl" and the "eighteen objects of a dhuta,"[27] including willow branches, soap, a water bottle, a mat, a monastic stick, an incense burner, and a water filter.

The eating implement a monastic uses is referred to as "the vessel that corresponds to one's needs." This means that one should know moderation and not be too greedy. According to the *Sutra of the King Fanmonan* [*Fanmonan Guowang Jing*], "Taking food and drink should be like taking medicine by a person who is ill. A person should not covet it after being cured." The *Connected Discourses of the Buddha* teaches, "One should always be mindful to eat moderately, which means eat sparingly, digest quietly, and thereby preserve life." The *Sutra of the Teachings Bequeathed by the Buddha* [*Fo Yijiao Jing*] advises, "Treat all food and drink like medicine. They can be beneficial and harmful; take in moderation to sustain the body and eliminate hunger and thirst."

A healthy approach to consuming food is to follow the "five contemplations at meal time": 1) by considering the work required to produce the food, I shall be grateful to its source; 2) reflecting on my own conduct, I shall deserve this offering if it accords with morality; 3) I shall guard my mind cautiously from being overly desirous; 4) to cure the ailment of hunger, I shall consume this food as medicine; and 5) to tread on the spiritual path, I shall accept this offering (*Monastic Regulations of Baizhang Revised by the Emperor Shunzong of Yuan Dynasty* [*Chixiu Baizhang Qing'gui*]).

If one is not greedy for material things, then one's spiritual life can rise to a higher level. The Buddha satisfied his hunger with sesame and wheat; the honored Mahakasyapa dwelled amid graves; Master Niaoke lived in a nest in a tree; Damei Fachang[28] wore clothes made of lotus leaves and ate pine nuts; the Sixth Patriarch[29] ate only vegetables, even when they were cooked with meat; and traveling monastics ate whatever was given to them. Amid the mountains and forests, they ate one meal a day and possessed nothing but the clothes on their backs and their alms bowls. With such freedom and carefree minds, could you call them poor? By contrast, can you call those people who live in high-rise apartments, drive luxury cars, and have servants rich when they spend their days in the pursuit of money and constantly worry about the fluctuation of the stock market? Can you say that those who possess loads of cash and acres of good land but who are stingy and never satisfied rich? Therefore, those who are rich in material goods are not necessarily rich, and those who lack such wealth are not necessarily poor. Wealth and poverty are not determined by money or material goods.

Although Buddhism does not direct much attention to materialism, most people still need some material goods to add comfort and dignity to life. If the main shrine of a temple is not imposing and majestic, how can it attract more people to come and pay homage to the Buddha and bodhisattvas? If a Buddhist statue is lacking in solemnity, who would respect it? It is precisely because the Western Pure Land is paved with "gold" and filled with "bejeweled" towers, so stately and majestic, that people are attracted to it and desire to be reborn there.

One can demand a simple life, but cannot apply this standard to others. Although Buddhism stresses the simple life, monasteries are built to house many for the night. It is as Du Fu[30] said in his "Thatched Hut Poem":

> Thousands of large halls,
> to shelter the world's poor scholars
> and bring smiles to their faces.

Although Buddhism admonishes us against material desire and is opposed to excessive indulgence in material pleasure, in this society, the moderate enjoyment of material culture is in accord with moral living. Yet practicing ascetics who hope to subdue their wills by tempering their material desires are also to be commended. In the monastic life, for example, when the master dies, his/her belongings are given to his/her disciples. One garment can be handed down for generations. I have experienced this myself over the years of my own monastic life. If we can distance ourselves from material things, then we are not slaves to them. That is why the *Diamond Sutra* [*Vajracchedika Prajna Paramita Sutra*] tells us not to dwell in the six dusts—form, sound, smell, taste, touch, and objects. The five desires and the six dusts are filled with defects and afflictions; once mired therein, it is difficult to extricate oneself. The *Collection of Great Treasures* asserts, "Riches, lust, and position are impermanent and last but a short time. The wise do not pursue momentary pleasures but diligently seek the most wonderful Buddha wisdom." The *Flower Ornament Sutra* [*Avatamsaka Sutra*] also notes, "The Dharma of eternal happiness, gentleness, and patience is to be found amid loving-kindness, compassion, joy, and equanimity."[31] We can find our path in life only by taming our material desires and taking delight in seeking the Dharma; and by being happy, gentle, and patient as well as possessing loving-kindness, compassion, joy, and equanimity.

Our lives are intertwined with material things. When it comes to food, clothing, shelter, and transportation, in which case can we forsake material things? In which case do we not form some relationship with material things? In life we cannot do without material things, and for this reason some people are willing to become slaves to them. However, the fact of the matter is that there is no need in life to exclusively pursue pleasure and riches. Instead of being a slave to money, a person should seek to enhance the appeal and flavor of life. Beautifying one's household surroundings, for example, can give us enjoyment. People can add to the charm of life by diligently sweeping their yards every day, by cleaning their houses and windows, by making their homes cozy, and by cultivating their gardens. Occasionally getting away to a scenic area with friends will also add a little spice to life. We can also give life more essence by immersing ourselves in work or nature, or by experiencing the way a flower blooms, a mountain landscape provides enjoyment, a bridge joins people, a tree gives shade, or a spring quenches thirst. We should strive for a lifestyle that gives value to life.

In summary, a person must live, just as a pig, horse, cow, or sheep must live. Even insects and other creatures must live. But the spice of life is different for each. People today like to enjoy name-brand clothes, jewelry, and popular makeup. Being thin is in vogue, and people like to make themselves over. However, true beauty is impressive, solemn, and composed yet carefree; it comes naturally from within. The *Sutra on the Treasury of Truth with Parables* [*Dharmapadavadana Sutra*] expresses this idea, "Wisdom without anger is uprightness." Life will have quality only if one strives to change one's personality, habits, ideas, and relationships, making the good better as well as improving, correcting, and beautifying the mediocre.

Thus, from the perspective of Humanistic Buddhism, life must be brought in line with the Dharma. This means that in addition to love and money, life must include the ideals of compassion, creating affinities, happiness, and kindness, as well as the Dharmas of reason and patience. Life will be richer with the Dharma than if one only possesses money and love.

On Emotions

the Way of Love and Affection

Where does life come from? As explained by the "twelve links of dependent origination," life originates from "love." Love and affection are the roots of life, hence the expression, "If one is not deeply attached to love, one will not be reborn on earth." My parents love one another, and I love my parents. The seeds of so much love and enmity lead to birth in the world of human beings. Love also leads to rebirth in samsara for kalpas. The *Sutra of Illuminating Light* articulates this idea: "People are deluded on account of ordinary love and kindness and are unable to rid themselves of passion and desire; thus love and sorrow grow, like water overflowing a pool."

Due to the ties of love, the wheel of samsara turns. Because human beings have feelings, they are termed "sentient beings." Even so, "Dharma is not good and bad; good and bad are dharmas." If one loves inappropriately, love can be like a rope that binds us, making freedom impossible for our bodies and minds. Ordinary love is like a pillory that holds us fast, denying our release. Ordinary love is like being blind, enveloping us in darkness and ignorance. Ordinary love is like a sea of bitterness in which we capsize and are lost.

However, "Purified love is compassion, and elevated love is wisdom." If love can be elevated to compassion, then "loving kindness will extinguish anger, and compassion will eliminate thoughts of harming others" (*Sutra of Bodhisattva Stages* [*Bodhisattvabhumi Sutra*]). The *Gradual Discourses of the Buddha* [*Ekottarikagama Sutra*] states, "All Buddhas manifest great compassion, and with the power of great sympathy spread benefits to all sentient beings." Compassion is the untiring motivation used by the Buddhas and bodhisattvas to liberate sentient beings. If people could treat each other compassionately, then love would be like sun in the winter, melting snow and ice. It can inspire truth, goodness, and the beauty of human nature; love is a force that can encourage us to rise to greater heights.

For this reason, Buddhism does not necessarily reject feelings; it advocates that feelings be imbued with compassion, purified by reason, circumscribed by etiquette, and guided by wisdom. Buddhism encourages love and intimacy between husband and wife, respect and forgiveness between parents and children, as well as care and cooperation among friends. Buddhism goes further by asking us to practice "unconditional loving-kindness and great compassion toward all," and also to elevate our personal feelings of love to compassion for all sentient beings. For example, the Buddha sat quietly in the middle of the road to prevent King Virudhaka from invading his homeland (fas. 26, *Gradual Discourses of the Buddha*). He loved his blind disciples and looked after ill bhiksus (*Vinaya*), and threaded the needle for Aniruddha (fas. 31, *Gradual Discourses of the Buddha*). The Jataka tales tell stories of "slicing one's flesh to feed a hawk, offering one's body as food for a tiger" and the like.

The Commentary on the *Main Mahayana Doctrines* [*Dacheng Baoyao Yi Lun*] says: "All sentient beings will be attached to love, and by reason of love commit wrongdoings and fall into evil. If sentient beings can give rise to compassion and not be attached to love, they will be born in the upper realms for not creating unwholesome causes. Furthermore, if they can reject all passions and concentrate on giving alms and doing other good deeds, with the Dharma and the good working in unison, the bodhisattva path can be cultivated to complete one's life." That is why the *Nirvana Sutra* proclaims, "Loving-kindness, compassion, joy, and equanimity are the transformation of the Tathagata, and they lead to liberation."

Compassion is love elevated. The Buddha's propagation of the Dharma to help others is love; his teachings and instructions for happiness are also love. Avalokitesvara Bodhisattva's great compassion and loving-kindness, rescuing people from hardships and difficulty, are all love. Love helps us, gives us respect and freedom, and makes life easier. Love is beauty, goodness, and truth; love is pure. The essence of Buddhism is loving-kindness, compassion, and pure love.

The *Sutra on Contemplation of the Buddha of Infinite Life* asserts, "Great compassion is the heart of the Buddha. Unconditional compassion is used to help sentient beings." According to the *Treatise on the Perfection of Great Wisdom* [*Mahaprajnaparamita Sastra*], "A mother, in her compassion, cares for her baby even though it dirties her. Because of her great love, she does not become angry and has sympathy because of her baby's innocence. A bodhisattva treats sentient beings in the same manner."

The bodhisattva cares about all sentient beings without distinction, whether they are family or not. For this reason, we should learn from all Buddhas and bodhisattvas to broaden and free love from its narrowest meaning of loving ourselves and our family to loving everyone in society, our country, and throughout the world. Through compassion we must expand the scope of love, purifying it through wisdom, respecting all that we love, and making sacrifices to fulfill our love. If there can be love and closeness among all people, how wide the world and universe would be!

In terms of marriage, the marriage of man and woman is the elevation, perfection, and unity of love. However, love is not unidirectional; love means that people should attempt to understand one another and to take the love they feel for a person and broaden it to include all sentient beings. The Confucians used to say that, "If a person feels sorry for a moth, he/she will not harm it; if one pities a mouse, one will leave it a little food." Buddhism expresses the same idea thusly, "If one treats animals, insects, and the downtrodden with the same compassion one has for a child, then one will pity them and provide food with which to revive them. Never will one use a knife or club to deprive them of their lives" (*Sutra of Buddha's Discourse on the Four Matters Requested by Ananda* [*Fo Shuo Anan Si Shi Jing*]).

Love is reciprocal. True love means helping and blessing the beloved. Love is not owning, but rather offering. Small love means loving that which is related to oneself; great love means loving that which is related to others. True love means loving the truth, the nation, the world, justice, and peace among peoples. The saying, "Life is really precious; the value of love is even greater," expresses the value of sentiment and righteousness, great affection and love, and a sense of great compassion and loving-kindness. A person can lose everything, but not compassion and loving-kindness.

In today's society, many people misuse and defame love. For example, in the name of love, some people lust after women and rape them; they steal and corrupt for the love of money; and commit crimes and violate the rights of others for the love of things that are not theirs. Love can harm others as well as oneself and can be the cause of grievous wrongdoing.

In truth, love is the origin of wrongdoing and the root of the cycle of birth and death. Although birth and death come from love, love is like water—it can sink or float a ship. Although a person can be misled by love, love can also improve people. When the Buddha was in the world, Matangi[32] was enamored of the honored Ananda. However, thanks to the skillful teaching of the Buddha, she realized that "Ordinary love is the root of suffering" (*Lankavatara Sutra*). When Utpalavarna[33] (Lotus Blossom Girl) was in the world of human feelings, she was injured and sought revenge by toying with love. Later, under the tutelage of Maudgalyayana, she finally understood that "Inappropriate love is the origin of suffering" and was reformed.

Love guides ethics and provides order. It is love that binds people together and provides order to the relationships between father and mother, husband and wife, sons and daughters, and friends. If a person has no love for father and mother, husband and wife, or children, can they love all sentient beings? Some people treat life so lightly, for example, by committing suicide and destroying themselves. If one does not love oneself, how can one love others? For this reason, the *Flower Ornament Sutra* tells us, "Love others as thyself; lead thyself by following others."

With love there is strength; with love there is hope. This is because love is an instinct, common to human beings and all living things. Buddhism will not deny or object to love as long as it is in accord with the law, morality, and the laws of human ethics. Buddhism neither approves nor rejects love. This is especially true of Humanistic Buddhism, which advocates the Middle Way for life. Love must be purified with compassion and guided by wisdom. Love must be accomplished with good and beauty; love must be supported by moral behavior. Life stems from love; we must add dignity and beauty to life with pure, true, and compassionate love.

On Society

the Way of Oneself and Others

Human beings are social animals. In the home, at school, and in society, humans need to have contact with one another. Interpersonal relations are an important facet of life today. Many of the difficulties people face these days are due to a lack of harmony in their relationships with others. People cannot cultivate themselves if they do not know how to treat others appropriately, a failing which sows the seeds of discord and leads to conflict.

Our relations with others are based on causes and conditions. Positive causes and conditions bear positive fruit; negative causes and conditions bring negative retribution. However, most people do not comprehend this relationship. They avoid helping one another; they cannot stand it if someone is smarter, taller, or bigger than themselves; and they do everything they can, arguing and fighting, to defeat and beat others. As soon as a person compares himself/herself to others, arguing over every little thing, then everything becomes a question of advantages and disadvantages. Because of this, even if people are as close as family and as affectionate as husband and wife, conflict is unavoidable.

The Buddhist sangha is itself a society. The meaning of the word "sangha" is "harmonious group." Although the Buddha stressed individual cultivation, he also established the sangha, indicating that he considered relationships between the individual and society a serious matter. In Buddhism there is the expression: "Prosperity in the monastic community occurs when there are no conflicts." Only when people are in harmony can they exist without conflict. The *Taking Refuge in the Triple Gem* [*San Guiyi Wen*] states: "I take refuge in the Sangha, wishing that all sentient beings lead the public in harmony, without obstructions." The words "lead the public in harmony" simply mean "to get along." The sangha normally relies upon the "six harmonies" to ensure harmony among people. The six points are: 1) physical unity by living together, 2) verbal unity by not criticizing others, 3) mental unity through shared joy, 4) moral unity through upholding the same precepts, 5) doctrinal unity in views, and 6) economic unity through sharing. The emphasis on unity is the reason the six harmonies are also referred to as the "six points of reverent harmony in the monastery."

In describing the Western Pure Land, the *Amitabha Sutra* mentions, "All excellent people will congregate there." The reason for this is harmony, harmony being the Pure Land. If a family is harmonious, that family will be happy; if a community is harmonious, that community will be peaceful. Subhuti was considered to be the best exponent of emptiness because of his realization of the *arana-samadhi*,[34] in which there is no dispute or distinction between self and others. The *Vinaya* also emphasizes harmony. It contains seven rules for settling disputes among monastics, which serve as standards for harmony in the sangha.

Buddhism is a religion that focuses on human beings. The Dharma provides solutions to nearly every human problem. For example, the *Gradual Discourses of the Buddha* provides methods for handling disputes between oneself and others. It cautions people not to slander others or take notice of their faults but rather to examine oneself and one's own conduct to determine whether or not one is correct.

Everyone hopes to have an exemplary reputation, but some people strive too hard for it. They do not hesitate to praise themselves while disparaging others. In their excessive criticism of others, it is not only easy to establish harmful causes with others, but also to fall into telling lies, ironically giving themselves a negative reputation. In discussing what must be done to earn an exemplary reputation, the *Sutra on the Principles of Six Paramitas* [*Liu Boluomiduo Jing*] teaches, "Do not disparage others and praise yourself; by not making distinctions between the self and others, one will earn a good name."

We should also keep in mind what the *Sutra of Illuminating Light* says: "Do not repay hatred with hatred; eventually, it must stop." If hatred is repaid with hatred, there will be no end. Our only choice is to reciprocate with virtue, and in this way we can cut off the roots of enmity. For example, Devadatta always opposed the Buddha and on several occasions sought to harm him. One day Devadatta became ill, and all the physicians were powerless to help him. Then the Buddha himself came to see him and looked after him with great concern. The Buddha's exemplary behavior is, in the words of the *Sutra on the Principles of Six Paramitas*, "Not to recall others' negative deeds, but always to look at a person's positive side. The Buddha has wisdom that goes beyond distinctions; therefore, he is the most enlightened of human beings."

Most people want to be better than others, because they are concerned with distinctions such as victory and defeat, which give rise to endless struggles. The *Sutra on the Treasury of Truth* [*Dharmapada Sutra*] states, "Victory breeds contempt, while defeat begets self-contempt. By ridding oneself of the distinction between victory and defeat, disputes will end and one will be at peace." So, if a person can respect another's greatness and thereby support and help another find fulfillment, that person can turn sadness into peace and happiness.

People also tend to strive to possess more than others, often ignoring the needs of others. They seek a life of ease and dislike to work, single-mindedly pursuing their own happiness without considering the sufferings of others. Even worse, many people prefer to blame other people for their own mistakes, which is also a source of discord. If we can all acknowledge our mistakes and negative behavior without always blaming others, and take responsibility for our own actions, then relations among people will be harmonious and without contention. As the *Sutra on the Collection of Important Points on All Dharmas* [*Zhu Fa Jiyao Jing*] says, "In the face of a violent person's unreasonable behavior and slander, the wise will only speak the truth and through patience avoid trouble."

Communities today advocate watching out for and assisting one another, as well as strengthening relations among neighbors and caring for the aged. On this subject, the *Collection of Great Treasures* remarks, "If a bodhisattva lives among people, he/she should teach the Dharma wherever he/she lives, be it village, city, prefecture, or county. He/she should lead the disbelievers to faith and the unfilial to filial piety. If people listen to him/her and he/she can persuade the stingy to give alms, those who break the prohibitions to uphold the precepts, the angry to be patient, the lazy to be diligent, those with restless minds to be calm, and the foolish to be wise, then the poor will have alms, the sick will have medicine, the defenseless will be protected, the homeless will have shelter, and the helpless will have assistance."

In any group, the most capable are those who can promote harmony, while those who are incapable often cause strife. If people can smooth over their differences, then harmony can be achieved. Harmony comes with respect and forgiveness. As the *Flower Ornament Sutra* mentions, "When the Buddha spoke of the four means of embracing, all sentient beings in the ten directions were gladdened." The best way to harmonize human relations is to practice the four means of embracing: 1) give charity, 2) utter kind words, 3) act altruistically and beneficently, and 4) cooperate and adapt oneself to others. When we give charity, it makes no difference whether it is money and wealth or strength and words; it can gladden all and benefit our interactions with others. Praising, helping, and treating others equally are wonderful ways to handle our day-to-day affairs. The Buddhist sutras teach us to form broad ties of good causes and conditions, which means we should not violate the rights of others nor let them down; instead we should endeavor to create beneficial conditions for others, because in doing so we create beneficial conditions for ourselves. Only by not violating the rights of others can we ensure harmonious relations.

The relations between oneself and others are two sides of the same coin and are produced by mutually existing causes and conditions. Each person is just one small part of the world. In addition to myself, there is you; in addition to you, there is him or her; and in addition to the three of us, there is everyone else.

Good relations between people in which there is help and fulfillment are a great blessing. Envy and rancor between people mean great unhappiness. The requisites for establishing positive relationships with others are mutual respect, forgiveness, understanding, and assistance. If one person cannot make allowances for another, then problems will arise.

In summary, disharmony between oneself and others is the cause of strife and injustice. Only by putting oneself in another's shoes and by treating others as you would have them treat you can human relations achieve harmony. Only by being able to see things from another's point of view can there be harmony among all.

On
Loyalty and Filial Piety

the Way of Establishing Oneself

There is a Chinese saying: "A loyal minister is a filial son." A minister who is loyal to the state is certainly a filial son. A person who is filial to his/her parents will be loyal to the state. Loyalty and filial piety form the basis for running one's home, governing the state, and bringing peace to the world. The first line in the *Principles for Youth* states: "Loyalty and courage are the foundation of patriotism." The second line proclaims: "Filial piety is the foundation for running one's home." Thousands of years of Chinese culture and history have taught Chinese people how to be loyal and filial. That is why when a family produces a loyal minister or filial son, everyone in the village takes pride. By the same token, a disloyal minister or an unfilial son will be the object of contempt and will find it difficult to live anywhere.

In the past, most people believed that a Buddhist monastic was running away from or fleeing the world and that he/she was unable to fulfill his/her duties of loyalty. However, Buddhists are the same as Confucians in terms of the importance they attach to interpersonal relations, the three bonds (relations between ruler and subject, father and son, and husband and wife), and especially the practice of loyalty and filial piety. The *Explanation of the Vimalakirti Sutra* [*Jing Ming Jing Guanzhong Shi Chao*] teaches, "Loyalty is to love one's master or superior; filial piety is to love one's parents." The *Essential Points of Buddhism* [*Shishi Yao Lan*] states, "A nation with a king and ministers will have peace. That is why a humane king is a source of happiness for all sentient beings. Those who work for the Dharma, at home or in the monastery, all look to the nation for support, progress, and help in spreading the Way. Without the power of a king, nothing can be achieved, the Dharma will be extinguished, and it is impossible to benefit sentient beings." This is why the *Sutra on the Contemplation of the Mind* teaches that there are four types of kindness that should be prayed for day and night: "the kindness of parents, the kindness of all sentient beings, the kindness of a ruler, and the kindness of the Triple Gem."

In addition, according to the *Sutra of Miscellaneous Treasures* [*Samyuktaratnapitaka Sutra*], the Buddha offered ten similes for teaching people how to be loyal and kind to a kingdom's ministers. He also told rulers that they should love and protect the people as well as be loyal to them. The sutra describes it thus, "A king is like a bridge, a safe crossing for everyone; he is like a scale, fairly balanced for all; he is like a road, good for sacred pursuits; he is like the sun, shining over the world; he is like the moon, fresh and cooling to all; he is like a father and mother, nurturing and kind; he is like heaven, overarching all; he is like the earth, supporting everything; he is like fire, eradicating all that is negative; and he is like water, irrigating the four directions."

If a minister of state embodies such benevolence, morality, and virtue, the people will naturally serve and be loyally devoted to him. By the same token, the king and all officials should do their best to love and protect the people and do everything for their happiness. Loyalty is a relationship that is based on mutual respect, a relationship of equality. The *Nirganthra Sutra* states that a country's rulers should do eight things to demonstrate that they are loyal to their subordinates: 1) treat all sentient beings as if they were their own beloved children, 2) treat all bad sentient beings as if they were their own ill children, 3) always be compassionate toward suffering sentient beings, 4) show joy at the happiness of sentient beings, 5) protect those sentient beings who are hateful from wrongdoing, 6) be doubly protective of friends and relatives, 7) treat nourishment like medicine, and 8) not regard themselves as superior.

The Buddha believed that the ideal for doing one's duty as a subject was for benevolent rulers and their respectful ministers to love one another and cooperate, and that the rulers should not instill fear in those beneath them or struggle with one another for ulterior motives. Monastics and the disciples of the Buddha from ancient times have worked for the safety of their countries, and have never been second to anyone in being loyal and steadfastly patriotic. In the Song Dynasty, for example, Emperor Huizong and Emperor Qinzong[35] were taken captive during the upheaval of Jingkang.[36] Emperor Kang set up court south of the Yangtze River and enlisted the service of Chan Master Fadao[37] in military planning and the collection of essential food supplies. The Master made a great contribution to the future stability of the nation south of the Yangtze River. During the An Lushan Rebellion[38] in the Tang Dynasty[39] and the subsequent collapse of the economy, Master Shenhui[40] sold ordainment certificates to help the army financially and thus calm the mutinous troops. These are just a few examples of Buddhist loyalty to the country during times of disaster and upheaval.

In the Hall of Great Wisdom at Fo Guang Shan is a memorial for highly esteemed monastics in remembrance of the Venerable Zongyang[41] from Qixia Temple[42] near Nanjing. In the years prior to the creation of the Republic, he joined the alliance led by Dr. Sun Yat-sen and helped raise funds to complete the revolution. The letters between him and Dr. Sun Yat-sen are preserved today.

In addition to the displays of loyalty to the nation by monastics throughout history, Sakyamuni Buddha himself once blocked King Virudhaka from invading his homeland by sitting down in the middle of the road under the boiling sun. Three times the King advanced, and three times the Buddha blocked his way. Clearly, the Buddha, like all people, loved his country.

The Buddha was not only a loyal subject, but he also stressed filial piety. When the Buddha's father, Suddhodana, passed away, the Buddha served as one of the pallbearers for his father's coffin at the funeral (*Sutra on the Nirvana of King Suddhodana Discoursed by the Buddha*). In order to repay his mother, Mahamaya, for giving him life, the Buddha used his spiritual powers to ascend to the Trayastrimasa Heaven,[43] where he spent three months delivering the *Sutra on Buddha's Ascension to the Trayastrimsas Heaven to Discourse the Dharma to His Mother* for her benefit. In order to repay the kindness of Mahaprajapati, his aunt and foster mother, he opened the Dharma gate of expedient compassion, permitting five hundred women of the Sakya clan[44] to renounce the world and become nuns. It is for this reason that there are bhiksunis in the sangha today. In order to fulfill the honored Maudgalyayana's filial request to rescue his mother from the realm of hungry ghosts, the Buddha delivered the *Ullambana Sutra*, and thereby established a means by which later generations of monastics could express their filial piety. Throughout the history of China, there have been countless monastics who have performed moving deeds of filial piety, all of which serve to demonstrate the profound filial piety inherent in Buddhism.

Many Buddhist scriptures such as the famous *Sutra of the Past Vows of the Earth Store Bodhisattva* [*Ksitigarbhapranidhana Sutra*], the *Ullambana Sutra*, and the *Sutra on the Difficulty of Repaying the Kindness of Parents* promote filial piety. Examples of Buddhist filial piety can be found throughout the Buddhist Canon. The *Brahma Net Sutra*, for example, says, "Other names for filial piety are precepts and control." Being filial means obeying one's parents; it also means upholding the precepts, not violating the rights of others, and controlling one's own behavior. This is a form of filial piety to all sentient beings.

For Buddhism, the word "loyalty" means absolute sincerity, to make a steady effort, being mindful and virtuous, and remaining consistent from beginning to end. When loyalty was mentioned in the past, most people believed it meant serving the ruler and being a loyal subject of the state. Actually, the meaning of the word "loyalty" should be broadened to include the loyalty between husband and wife, among friends, and even loyalty to one's job. One must stand behind one's promises and firmly uphold one's beliefs. If you decide to raise a kitten or puppy, you must do so without wavering. That is also an example of loyalty.

A person who is loyal will not forsake what is right for what is profitable, nor will he/she be fickle. Loyalty means seeing one's own affairs to a conclusion. For example, a primary school student must complete his/her elementary-school education; the same goes for a middle-school or college student. If you waste your time, you are not being loyal to yourself.

Loyalty is a kind of trust, a kind of dedication. It also means sticking to what is good. We must choose that which deserves our loyalty. The expression, "Birds know instinctively how to choose a branch on which to perch; a loyal minister chooses a ruler and serves him" means that the object of our loyalty must be good, worthy, and right, as well as benevolent and just. It is immoral to be loyal to the licentious or deceitful. Therefore, any discussion of loyalty must include the heart, the right, the good, and the beautiful.

Loyalty is an expression of benevolence, compassion, and faith. The expression "being loyal to the ruler and loving the country" equates loyalty with love. If you are loyal to someone, then you must certainly love him/her, and if you love someone, then you must certainly be loyal to him/her. The past president of the Republic of China, Chiang Kai-shek, advocated loyalty to our leaders, the nation, and our own responsibilities and honor. He personally felt that it was most important to be loyal to one's leader. By contrast, Buddhism advocates, "relying on the Dharma and not the person." Therefore, in doing one's duty by the Dharma, one should be loyal to the system and the group, not just to an individual.

This is especially true since loyalty is reciprocal. A minister must be loyal to the leader, but the leader must also be loyal to the minister. However, it should be noted that in loyalty, there is both positive and negative loyalty, as well as correct and incorrect loyalty. This deserves more explanation. In loyalty, there is no gain or loss, no specified duration of time, and no consideration of advantages or disadvantages. If something or someone is deserving of loyalty, then I will still give my loyalty, even if it is not to my benefit. Only this can truly be called loyalty.

There is an absolute, undivided, complete, and focused sense to the word "loyalty." When one can fulfill one's responsibilities with an undivided focus and without considering success or failure, then one can be said to be loyal. But doing one's duty does not necessarily mean sacrificing one's life for nothing. If each one of us can stand by our principles, do our jobs, and fulfill our responsibilities, then we can be considered loyal. If everyone in society can work diligently without slacking off or cheating, then everyone is doing his/her duty to society. As Buddhists, if we can all apply the Dharma to purify hearts and to improve society and the mood of the people, then we are doing our duty by society.

Since ancient times, the establishment of Buddhist temples has allowed people to light a lamp in their hearts, eliminating darkness, foolishness, and ignorance. This light of wisdom has provided a framework for the mind and armor for the spirit. In this way, Buddhism has been able to fulfill its duty to society. As followers implement the teachings of the Buddha, they transform ruthlessness and tyranny with compassion, eliminate anger and hatred with patience, and overcome stubbornness with wisdom. In this way, Buddhism is doing its duty to all sentient beings. Therefore, the meaning of loyalty is not necessarily restricted to some narrow sense of serving one person, or of respecting and worshipping one thing. Loyalty in its broadest sense means to serve all sentient beings. In the family, one must loyally fulfill one's obligations to one's spouse and children; in society one must be responsible to the group, the company, and one's superiors. A person must deal with others in a just and upright fashion. In the pursuit of ideals, one must be loyal to one's own principles. In life, the virtue of loyalty is integral to our relationships. A sincere and loyal person is always a beacon of light in this world. Loyalty is a virtue that has a profound and enormous impact on our growth as individuals.

Loyalty and filial piety are often placed on a par with one another. Loyalty is trust, dedication, and study; filial piety is respect, love, and protection. Most people believe that filial piety is merely taking care of one's parents. Even birds and beasts understand this. Taking care of one's parents is the most basic form of filial piety. However, in addition to being filial to one's parents, a person should also be filial to the members of one's extended family, and even go a step further and be filial to one's friends and all sentient beings.

Today, those who care for the aged and raise the young do so out of a sense of filial piety. Compassion and joyful giving are fulfilled through a filial heart. We not only want to be filial toward our parents, but also to our neighbors, our compatriots, and all of humanity. We not only want to be filial toward our elders but also toward the physically handicapped, the aging, and the infirm.

"Filial piety" is the outward expression of love. It is the expression of our true feelings toward country and family. It is also something that we should have for others and is integral to all ethical relationships. Filial piety provides order among generations, a virtue that is passed from one generation to the next. It is an expression of the sincere gratitude we feel toward life and the repaying of kindness without regrets or complaints. Buddhism holds that it is "small filialness" to do things for oneself and loved ones; "middle filialness" is to do things for one's family and relatives; "great filialness" is to do things for one's country. The *Ullambana Sutra* states, "When the disciples of the Buddha practice filial devotion, they should constantly remember to make offerings to their parents and appreciate their parents from the past seven lives."[45] The Buddha also taught his disciples that they should not only respect their worldly parents, but also respect their parents from the past seven lives, as well as the parents of all sentient beings. For this reason, "filialness" is not limited to devotion to one's parents here and now. Filial piety should begin with one's own parents, then progress "to being a parent and a child to all," and finally be expanded to include all of society and ultimately all sentient beings. One should not only be filial to one's own parents, but also favor the parents of all sentient beings and direct all of one's efforts to solving the afflictions of living beings. The *Diamond Sutra* [*Vajracchedika Prajnaparamita Sutra*] states, "All beings, whether they are born from eggs, wombs, moisture, or transformation; whether they have form or are without form; or whether they have perception or non-perception, or whether they have perception nor non-perception, I will lead them to the liberation of parinirvana." Only in this way can one be considered filial to all sentient beings.

If we say that loyalty pertains to the relationship between the state, the people, and ourselves then filial piety applies to our relationships with our relatives and other people and creatures. Chinese culture advocates the "three bonds in human relations,"[46] but the focus is clearly on filial piety. Filial piety is central but must be expressed more broadly. The filialness one has for the state is loyalty; the filialness one has for one's brothers is brotherly love; the filialness one has for one's friends is virtue;

and the filialness one has for all sentient beings is benevolence. This is especially true when we speak of filial piety today; it is to actively care for our parents, to relieve the elderly of loneliness, and even to solve the problems facing the elderly. Only this can be considered "great filialness."

Loyalty and filial piety are complementary. A loyal dog serves its master to repay his/her love and protection; a minister serves his/her leader to thank him/her for recognition and employment. If we wish others to treat us with loyalty, then we must first express our sincerity and loyalty to them.

A gatha says, "Do not look for the Buddha on faraway Vulture Peak; Vulture Peak is right there in your mind. Each of us has Vulture Peak within; we should look toward our own Vulture Peak to practice our cultivation." Loyalty and filial piety are feelings that arise from our hearts and intuitive knowledge, as well as a kind of love and virtue. Loyalty and filial piety are the ethical ties that bind us together in our relationships. Only by expressing the spirit of loyalty and filial piety, by allowing loyalty and filial piety as well as compassion and love to spread throughout time and place, can society become more orderly and our families happier.

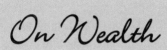

On Wealth

the Way of Financial Management

Everyone must have a job. Through hard work and disciplined management of one's affairs, one can enjoy an abundance of life's necessities and a peaceful existence. Only then can a person engage in doing good deeds. That is what is meant by the expression: "First life's necessities have to be attended to, then the rites and music will flourish."

In the past, many practitioners of early Buddhism emphasized cultivation over wealth. They sought to live plain, simple lives, and advocated poverty and honesty. They believed that cultivation was possible only with simplicity and that the Way was to be found therein. However, if one examines the Mahayana sutras such as the *Amitabha Sutra*, one will find scenes of unimaginable wealth: the Western Pure Land is paved with gold, and the palaces and towers are made of seven precious gems. The bodhisattvas wear jeweled crowns and necklaces of precious stones, extremely solemn and magnificent. Therefore, in practicing the Dharma, we do not necessarily have to stand aloof from the world by living a life of poverty and hardship. Honesty is all that is needed. Buddhism holds that lay devotees may have fame and accumulate wealth. In the words of the *Collection of Great Treasures*: "Lay bodhisattvas may accumulate wealth, but it must be done so in accordance with the Dharma." Once a person possesses wealth, he/she should "attend to his/her parents, husband or wife, and children, give charity to his/her personal friends, relatives, and good Dharma friends, and then give the gift of the Dharma." What this means is that as one makes a living, one must accumulate that which is right by working and living in accordance with the Noble Eightfold Path. The *Connected Discourses of the Buddha* teaches, "Ways to make a living include farming, doing business, herding cattle and sheep, and construction." For Buddhism, as long as one earns on one's own capital and diligently devotes oneself to making a living, all ways are legitimate, including farming, business, management, or interest-bearing investments.

By the same token, Buddhism disapproves of ill-gotten gains acquired by stealing, corruption, reneging on debts, appropriating another's money, embezzlement, taking by force, prospering through extortion, illegal business, deceiving investors, and profiteering. Buddhism condemns breaking the law, whether it is selling drugs or trafficking in human life, and improper jobs such as butchering or running a bar or gambling establishment; that is, any occupation that violates the Dharma—those that run counter to the precepts against killing, stealing, sexual misconduct, lying, or taking intoxicants and drugs.

The *Middle Length Discourses of the Buddha* [*Madhyamagama Sutra*] asserts that there are six inappropriate ways to make money: 1) making money by gaming; this includes gambling on sporting matches, tournaments, and in other facilities, 2) engaging in improper lines of work; this refers to those who ignore family duties, for example, by loitering about without proper employment, 3) getting drunk and engaging in excessive behavior; alcohol can cloud the mind, lead to excessive behavior, and is unproductive, 4) becoming friends with the impious for the purpose of earning a profit; by making bad friends, one will not make money but lose everything instead, possibly even one's life, 5) indulging in indecent pleasure; this includes those who waste themselves on song, dance, and prostitutes, and 6) being lazy in the pursuit of wealth; this refers to those who do not like to work and will use any excuse to avoid it.

These six inappropriate ways consume wealth rather than produce it. Not only do they result in the loss of wealth, health, and reputation in this life, but also unhappiness in future lives and not being reborn as a human being. Therefore, when we say *inappropriate* ways, we mean evil and unethical ways.

Once a person possesses wealth, then he/she must know how to handle it. This is an important issue. A gatha from the *Connected Discourses of the Buddha* states, "One fifth for food, two fifths for business, one fifth to save, and the remaining fifth for the poor." So, if you have a monthly income of three thousand US dollars, twelve hundred would go into your business, six hundred into the maintenance of your household, six hundred into your savings account, and the remaining six hundred returned to society as alms to support the poor.

In the *Collection of Great Treasures*, the Buddha tells us how to manage our wealth by using the example of King Prasenajit, who because of his great wealth had no need for financial planning. This being the case, he devised a tripartite plan for managing his wealth: he used one third for religious offerings, one third to assist the poor, and one third for the nation's resources. The *Nirvana Sutra* says that in addition to providing for daily needs, a person's wealth should be disposed of in four parts: one fourth for supporting one's parents and family, one fourth for servants, one fourth for friends and relatives, and one fourth for the country and monastics.

There are many kinds of wealth: wealth in the narrow and broad sense; tangible and intangible wealth; wealth in this life and in lives to come; personal and public wealth; material and spiritual wealth; as well as transitory and eternal wealth. Buddhism emphasizes eternal wealth over the transitory variety, wealth in lives to come over that of the present life. Wealth in the narrow sense of money is important, but even more important is wealth in the broad sense, which includes health, wisdom, personal relations, ability, trustworthiness, eloquence, prestige, achievement, history, character, and morality. These intangible forms of wealth are superior to more tangible forms. Buddhism places more emphasis on public wealth than on personal wealth. Examples of public wealth include roads, parks, rivers, public works, and even the protection of nature and all creatures in the universe. Buddhism also advocates enjoyment in lieu of possession, wisdom instead of money, satisfaction as opposed to desire, thought in place of material goods, and the development of a sense of universalism.

For Buddhism, then, true wealth is not necessarily money in the bank, real estate, dwellings, gold, or silver, all of which are prey to rulers, thieves, flood, fire, and wasteful children. These are things that an individual cannot possess alone. True wealth is the Dharma, faith, compassion, satisfaction, joy, modesty, personal relations, safety, health, wisdom, determination to strive for enlightenment, and the liberation of all sentient beings.

The Buddhist belief is that if wealth is to be accumulated in this life, we must develop a habit of saving, of putting away a little bit of our income each month. We should be like honey bees, busily going from flower to flower to collect nectar, drop by drop; making honey, making wealth. For this reason, the *Middle Length Discourses of the Buddha* tells us: "Starting small, wealth is accumulated much like honey bees collecting pollen among the flowers; wealth grows day by day until finally it cannot be depleted."

In the view of Buddhism, having or not having wealth is explained first by cause and effect and karmic retribution. Possessing wealth is the result of cultivating happiness and morality and broadly forming good ties. Also, one "must be able to use wealth instead of be used by it." This is in line with the Six Points of Reverent Harmony in the Sangha, which emphasizes "benefit and harmony for all," and is in complete accordance with the modern idea of sharing, glory, and enjoyment.

Buddhism views wealth as "neither good nor bad" and does not deny it. Money can be a poisonous serpent, but it can also be used to spread and practice the Dharma. According to the Buddhist scriptures, there have been wealthy believers such as the Elder Sudatta,[47] who donated the Jetavana to the sangha (*Sutra on the Distinguishing Merits and Virtues* [*Punya Vibhanga Sutra*]), and Visakha, who contributed "the four offerings for a monastic" (*Four Part Vinaya*). All of them won the praise of the Buddha. For this reason, Buddhism does not place undue emphasis on asceticism, because demanding a plain and simple life for oneself is moral, but to demand it of others is too harsh.

Money can provide the resources for studying the Way, and it is the basis for the propagation of Buddhism. Buddhist institutes, meditation halls, schools, hospitals, television stations, and magazines all require money. For this reason, money cannot be regarded entirely as a poisonous serpent. "Clean wealth," "good wealth," and "sacred wealth" are referred to in the Buddhist sutras as money used for good, for spreading the Dharma, and for benefiting sentient beings. The merit accrued through utilizing money in this way is greater by far than studying the Way in poverty. It is also wiser and more significant.

Therefore, one can have one's mind set on enlightenment and not necessarily have to study the Way in poverty. For the individual, Mahayana Buddhism advocates simple food and clothing, but wealth is necessary for temples and groups. The construction and decoration of temples–the red eaves, golden-tiled roofs, carved and painted beams, splendid and solemn pavilions, terraces, towers, and corridor after corridor–all require money, hence the term "Buddhist Pure Land." Actually, Buddhism is a pure and spiritual existence, a joyful and prosperous world.

Humanistic Buddhism should redefine the value of wealth. As long as it is clean wealth and in accordance with the right occupation and livelihood, then the more the better. As long as it is beneficial to the people, society, and the economy, and as long as the occupation–such as farming, manufacturing, business, or banking–adds to the happiness and prosperity of life, Buddhists should participate. Having money is not shameful, but poverty can lead to evil.

On
Long Life & Happiness
the Way of Ownership

Long life and happiness are sought by all; everyone hopes to be rich and honored, to live long, and to be happy. However, more often than not, obtaining both long life and happiness proves to be difficult. A person might be richer than the nation, yet die young, unable to enjoy it; another person might live to be as old as Methuselah, but be poor and down and out all his or her life. Only when the causes and conditions are complete can the blessings of long life and happiness be attained.

How can one cultivate the causes of long life and happiness? According to Buddhist beliefs, neither the heavens above, nor any authority on earth bestow upon us long life and happiness; instead, our own karma determines long life and happiness. We reap what we sow, if you will. A person's good behavior and actions will bring long life and limitless happiness, while bad behavior and actions will cut off the causes for long life and happiness. Buddhism speaks of five precepts. By not stealing, one will be happy; by not killing, one will have long life. In this way, upholding the five precepts leads to happiness and long life.

The *Sutra on the Eight Purification Precepts* [*Astangasamanvagata Sutra*] teaches that by receiving and upholding the eight purification precepts, one will be "happy beyond measure." The *Sutra on the Treasury of Truth* [*Dharmapada Sutra*] tells us that, "For the person who reveres and respects his or her elders, the four blessings–appearance, strength, longevity, and happiness–will naturally increase." The *Dharma Garden of Buddhism* also asserts that we will obtain long life and happiness if we practice seven types of charitable giving, which include: 1) erecting images of the Buddha and building monasteries, 2) planting orchards, 3) giving care and medicine to relieve the ailing, 4) providing ferries, 5) building roads and bridges, 6) lighting lamps, digging wells, and offering tea, and 7) providing restrooms. The *Sutra of the Great-Teacher King* [*Da Jiao Wang Jing*] states, "Happiness and long life are desired; they are attained when karma ripens. One should do good, respecting the Triple Gem of the Buddha, the Dharma, and the Sangha. Then, attaining the throne, one will be secure; becoming a minister, one will remain unharmed; and being born as a human being, one will live long." We can cultivate our blessedness in all fields of merit, such as by respecting the Triple Gem, parents, and teachers; teaching disciples; and helping the ill, the physically handicapped, and victims of disaster. There is a Buddhist saying:

> A good heart and a good life
>> Will bring riches and honor to a long life
> A good life and a bad heart
>> Will see blessings turn to disaster
> A good heart and a bad life
>> Will see disaster transformed into blessings
> A bad heart and a bad life
>> Will bring disaster and poverty
> The heart can change a life
>> Best remain on the road of benevolence
> Life is formed in the heart
>> A person creates his/her own fortune or misfortune
> Believing in destiny without cultivating the heart
>> And all will prove superficial and false
> Cultivating the heart upon hearing destiny call
>> One will be protected by heaven and earth

The karma of happiness and long life are inextricably linked to the cultivation and kindness of the heart. If we can form relationships with others and cultivate the causes for happiness and long life, then naturally happiness and longevity will follow suit. Knowingly doing bad, one may be able to achieve success one way or another and may enjoy a moment of pleasure, but disaster will follow quickly. For example, a person might obtain temporary happiness by stealing someone else's wealth, but later, after the crime is revealed and he or she is punished, it will be more like licking honey from a knife. Although the honey is sweet and tasty, the blade will prove cruelly painful. So, while good causes remain unmanifested, one must persevere in benevolence and compassion, and disaster will eventually turn to blessings.

The causes and effects that lead to happiness and long life are discussed in the sutras, but some people believe that they should pray to the gods, the bodhisattvas, and the Buddha instead. Their faith is built on a longing for having and taking more than they need. The *Sutra on the Treasury of Truth* tells us, "Seeking happiness by worshipping the gods, one waits for the rewards; getting no results, one would be better off respecting the sage." Simply having the desire for happiness and long life does not necessarily mean they will be obtained. If one does not cultivate the causes of happiness and long life, such desires will not come on their own. There is a saying: "Being born in heaven, one must have achieved the necessary causes and conditions, but one will not necessarily become an immortal by seeking to be one." What this means is that if we do not strive for happiness ourselves and we instead place the burden on the Buddha, we will not be living in accordance with the law of karma. This would be like placing a heavy stone in the water and expecting it to float, contrary to common sense. According to the *Longshu Extended Composition of Pure Land* [*Longshu Zeng'guang Jingtu Wen*], "By doing good in the present life, happiness and longevity will increase; by doing evil in this life, happiness and longevity will decrease." If our deeds and actions are in accordance with the Law of Cause and Effect, we should be able to enjoy the fruits of long life and happiness, and the dragon kings, devas, and gods will not be able to hide the fruits of our actions. It is like hot oil floating on water. Someone might ask the oil to sink, but it is impossible. Therefore, the attainment of happiness and long life cannot be manipulated. Even the gods have no control over our lives and deaths, our suffering and happiness. Everything is dependent upon whether we ourselves diligently sow the seeds of happiness and longevity.

Having sufficient happiness and longevity is something that most people hope for, especially the "five blessings that descend upon a house"–happiness, status, wealth, long life, and joy. These are what constitute happiness for most people. But if someone does in fact possess all five types of happiness, will life be perfect and without regrets? Is happiness in life limited to the five types? Everything has its cause and effect, and long life and happiness also have their own shortcomings and are not entirely without outflows. For example, people often comment to others with some envy, "you have a happy lot in life," but if you have "happiness" you naturally will have "worry." For example, having many children will also bring many troubles. When children are small, we worry about their health and growth. When they grow up, we worry about their success or failure. Even after they have a career and are married, we worry about their satisfaction at home and whether their careers are going smoothly. If our children are unfilial, our worries only increase. The more children, the more happiness and worries; the more wealth, the more worries seem to follow the good, the way a shadow follows a body. With money, one can enjoy all manners of sensual pleasure, but at times money can also bring us unexpected troubles.

"Happiness" and "worry" are as closely linked as a body is to its own shadow. "Longevity" and "old age" are inseparable as well. In Chinese culture, we often say: "May you live to be a hundred" and even "May you live to be one hundred and twenty." Perhaps someone who lives to the ripe age of one hundred and twenty is the envy of all, but if a person really did live that long, his/her children, eighty-year-old grandchildren, and sixty-year-old great-grandchildren may have all already passed away. Why live to that gray old age just to bury one's descendants? What would be the meaning of life to have lived so long?

Therefore, Buddhism does not necessarily consider that old age is all it is made out to be, or a goal that we ought to pursue. Nor does Buddhism deny the pursuit of long life and happiness. Buddhism advocates, "In pursuing happiness, pursue the happiness of wisdom; in pursuing long life, pursue a long life with more compassion." Happiness without wisdom is as difficult as driving a car that is missing a wheel, or flying with one wing. Only when happiness is combined with wisdom will there be merit. Only the happiness of wisdom will allow one to give that same happiness to all sentient beings. By the same token, to live a long life without doing good has no lasting significance for sentient beings. For this reason we should seek the happiness of wisdom and compassionate old age.

When one considers long life, it is important to keep in mind that there is the present life, the next life, as well as countless future lives. It is the same as the withering and fading of fruit and flowers–life will continue as long as the seeds are sown. Although the human body is a result of karma and subject to conditions–it has a beginning and an end–the value of life itself is not subject to conditions and is eternal. Thus, in pursuing long life, we should pursue infinite life.

"Infinite Life" is another name for Amithaba Buddha. He is also called "Infinite Light." Infinite life transcends time and space. If we can make limitless space and time the abode for our spirit, wisdom, and contributions, then will we not have infinite life? Thus, in addition to the life of this precious body, we should note some other forms of long life:

1) *The life span of an enterprise.* This includes establishing a business, creating a prosperous homeland, and extending benefits to all of society, such as by establishing companies and factories. They can be managed for several decades or even a century. It takes not only our entire lifetime but also those of our descendents to keep it going. This is the longevity of an enterprise.

2) *The life span of a culture.* The preciousness of human life is found in the transmission of culture, the words and deeds of our ancestors, and historical experience. These are all part of our precious cultural heritage. Chinese historical relics and records, including the Buddhist Canon all constitute the precious cultural life that Buddhist disciples must cherish.

3) *The life span of teachings.* Achieving virtue, rendering

meritorious service, and achieving immortality through one's ideas and sayings–these are some of the precious teachings of ancient scholars that are still being transmitted today. These teachings from the past are the inherited wisdom of humankind, a cultural treasure house. Books were written and ideas established by the ancients and later handed down. Culture is thus renewed like adding fuel to a fire. The life span of teachings transcends time and space; it is a life lived in the exchange of minds.

4) *The life span of faith.* The Chinese emphasize the idea of handing things down from one generation to the next. Actually, this includes more than just the continuity of life. An enterprise must be passed on, as must faith over generations, one lamp lighting the next. Each generation of Buddhist disciples passing on the wisdom of the Buddha is the life of faith.

5) *The life span of morality.* The ancients said, "The example is to be sought in the past." Sages throughout Chinese history have sacrificed themselves for benevolence and justice. The morality handed down by the ancients and cherished by later generations is the perfect achievement of virtue.

6) *The life span of wisdom.* A life of wisdom is a life of liberation and purity. Such a life includes joy, selflessness, compassion, and the limitless merit of wisdom. Buddhists should strive to fulfill the inexhaustible treasure house of life through diligent practice and self-improvement.

7) *The life span of merit.* Erecting halls, bridges, and Buddhist images; printing books on Buddhism; planting trees; offering food; and other meritorious deeds are acts to be cherished by later generations and blessings for which our descendants can be proud. The heritage of merit left by the monastic community has been to change and influence imperceptibly by practicing and upholding the Way. In addition to raising their own lives to a higher level, they also strengthen the faith of future generations of believers. This pure, immaterial merit is eternal.

8) *The life span of coexistence.* The ideals of caring for others and developing personal relations are deeply rooted in Buddhism. Today, this also includes loving and caring for the earth, protecting the environment, and cherishing natural resources. Allowing the environment and the causes of our coexistent life to continue means the continuation of the coexistence of time and space, enabling future generations to enjoy peace, happiness, and a collective life of ease.

Confucius said, "A person who hears about the Way has not lived in vain, even if he/she lives for only a day." For Confucius, the meaning of life was not related to status or pay, but rather rationally arriving at the Way and benefiting the world. The *Sutra on the Treasury of Truth* remarks, "Better to live one day pursuing the Dharma than one hundred years without the supreme truth." Though one might live to be the age of Methuselah, in the end, old age, sickness, death, and rebirth cannot be avoided. Happiness in the world is as rare as being a king or emperor, and in the end it all comes to naught. Therefore, when we seek happiness, we must strive for eternal happiness, life after life, and not the momentary happiness of this life. As the *Diamond Sutra* states, "the happiness of this life is limited, comes to an end, and has causes and outflows; eternal happiness is limitless and has no end or outflows, nor can it be stolen, burned, or lost."

People say, "One seldom lives to be seventy-years-old," but Zhang Qun once said, "Life begins at seventy." If you live to be one hundred and twenty, and you are extremely wealthy, how much do you really "have" and how much do you "enjoy"? Even if you "have" a hundred years, how much leisure time did you "enjoy"? Even if you "have" a high-rise apartment with thousands of lovely rooms, how many sweet dreams did you "enjoy"? Although you "have" a family, are your family members really close to you? Although you "have" many enterprises, can you rely upon them? Therefore, what you "have" in this world cannot necessarily all be "enjoyed" by you. Conversely, if you do not "have" something, it does not necessarily mean you cannot "enjoy" it.

For these reasons, the most important thing about life is to pass it in ease and happiness. Daily life needs order–early to bed, early to rise, a time to work, and a time to rest. It means maintaining a calm and happy state of mind and not being easily angered. One must be diligent in obtaining new knowledge and skills, establishing enterprises, serving society, and improving one's life. By enriching one's life, there will be no room for affliction. In this way, one can enjoy a happy life at ease.

Thus, in addition to managing time, fighting for time, and using time to benefit society and extend one's own life span, we should be diligent in creating lasting, beautiful language, good morals, incorruptible culture, illustrious enterprises, firm faith, pure wisdom, eternal virtue, and collective life. Only in this way can we truly "have" happiness and long life.

On
Maintaining Good Health
the Way of Medicine

The most precious thing in this world is not money, fame, power, or position; rather, it is health. Only with health can one enjoy the happiness of life. If a person does not have health, then his/her professional success, wealth, servants, and houses are all for naught–they are not his or hers. Therefore, the most important thing in life is staying healthy in body and mind.

"All dharmas arise due to causes and conditions, and all dharmas are extinguished due to causes and conditions." Between the arising and extinguishing of causes, birth, old age, sickness, and death are all unavoidable. Human beings rarely avoid getting sick. According to the *Sutra of the Buddha's Diagnosis* [*Fo Yi Jing*], people become ill for a number of reasons, including sitting for a long time without eating, exhaustion, excessive eating, anxiety, indulging in sensual pleasures, anger, not using the restroom, breathing incorrectly, and suppressing gas.

The *Path of Purification* [*Visuddhimagga*] points out eight reasons for illness: wind, phlegm, eating and drinking irregularly, unwholesome karma, injury, non-humans, ghosts, and mara.[48] The *Great Techniques of Stopping Delusion and Seeing Truth* [*Mohe Zhiguan*] mentions six reasons for illness: imbalance among the four elements, eating and drinking irregularly, disharmony in body and mind when meditating, ghosts getting the upper hand, harassment by evil spirits, and bad karma. As for the first three reasons, all one needs to do is adjust one's eating habits and reduce exposure to germs, then illness will be easy to treat or avoid. However, the latter three are related to an individual's karma. Only by paying respect to Buddhas, repenting, and cultivating happiness will one lessen the effects of illness.

All illnesses, then, can be reduced to one of two causes, the first of which is an imbalance among the four elements. The human body is composed of four elements. According to the third fascicle of the *Record of Buddhist Schools in India and Southern Asia* [*Nanhai Jigui Neifa Zhuan*], "When the body, which is composed of the four elements, becomes ill, it is usually due to overeating or overexertion." The *Condensed Techniques of Stopping Delusion and Seeing Truth* [*Xiao Zhi Guan*] mentions that each one of the four elements can produce a hundred and one illnesses, for a total of four hundred and four. When the earth element dominates, the body will be affected by lethargy and pain; when the water element dominates, food will not be digested properly, the stomach will ache, and there will be diarrhea; when the fire element dominates, the body will be racked with fever and going to the bathroom will be difficult; and when the wind element dominates, the lungs will be affected, breathing will be difficult, and vomiting is common.

Second, in addition to an imbalance among the four elements, the three poisons of greed, anger, and ignorance are also major causes of illness. The *Vilimakirti Sutra* asserts, "All of my present illnesses are the result of past false views. Afflictions and illnesses are produced because sentient beings cling to the self." The fourteenth chapter of the *Treatise on the Perfection of Great Wisdom* notes, "The effects of anger are the worst of the three poisons. Of the ninety-eight worries,[49] this is the most stubborn, and of all diseases of the mind, the most difficult to cure."

Venerable Master Zhizhe[50] believes that those who indulge in sexual pleasure will contract diseases of the liver; those who greedily enjoy sound will develop kidney diseases; those who long for fragrance will develop diseases of the lungs; those who love to eat excessively will develop illnesses of the heart; and those who are fond of touching things will develop diseases of the spleen. Clearly, following the Middle Way is good. Otherwise, craving sleep may lead to madness; cravings for rich, high-fat food, and carbohydrates may cause all sorts of chronic illnesses; a lack of exercise and high levels of noise will possibly lead to modern diseases, for example, cancer, and mental illness.

Modern physiologists believe that psychological responses such as anger, joy, anxiety, fear, sadness, and excitement can effect internal physiological changes, which, over time, can cause illnesses such as gastrointestinal ulcers and mental illness. One medical research report states: "When a person is unhappy, angry, or nervous, the brain will secrete noradrenalin, a toxic substance." In addition to diseases of the organs, sentient beings are also subject to psychological illnesses such as greed, anger, ignorance, and other mental illnesses. To cure the psychological illnesses of sentient beings, the Buddha spent a lifetime preaching the Tripitaka and the twelve sections of the Buddhist Canon, offering a prescription for the cure of all illnesses, physical and psychological. Hence, the scriptural analogies: "The Buddha is a doctor, the Dharma a prescription, the Sangha a nurse, and sentient beings the patients."

In addition to being a great doctor, able to heal the physical ailments of all sentient beings, the Buddha was also a great psychologist gifted in curing all manners of psychological ailments. For example, he expounded eighty-four thousand Dharma methods including the three studies, the six perfections, the four immeasurable states of mind, and the five contemplations. These Dharma methods[51] are all used for curing greed, anger, ignorance, and eighty-four thousand other illnesses that afflict sentient beings. The Buddha instructs the greedy to cure themselves with the concept of defilement; he instructs the angry to use compassion to cure themselves; and he instructs the ignorant to cure themselves with the concept of cause and condition. The Buddha is the world's greatest physician.

The *Gradual Discourses of the Buddha*, in addition to explaining the qualities of good physicians and nurses, also prescribes five Dharma methods for a patient to follow: 1) select the appropriate food, 2) eat at the right time, 3) keep in contact with a physician, 4) do not worry, and 5) be compassionate toward nurses. To stay healthy, the scriptures generally teach us to focus on these important factors:

1) *Right diet.* The *Nirgrantha Sutra* notes, "People who eat too much will become heavy and lazy. In this life and future lives, their bodies will suffer and they will always be sleepy; they will also afflict others; and being lethargic, awakening will be difficult. They should control their eating." Eating and drinking should be considered the same as taking medicine. Food is consumed for the nourishment it contains. So, when eating, one should keep in mind: more vegetables, less meat; more bland, less salt; more fruit, less sugar; and more chewing, less eating. Also, food should be consumed at regular times and in regular quantities. This is the first rule for staying healthy.

2) *Right occupation.* The right work is something positive, something that benefits society. Many people find work a hardship and filled with pressure. That is because they look at work simply as a way to make money, build a reputation, or for their own benefit, which is why they find it exhausting. The *Sutra of All Wisdom and Virtues* [*Yiqie Zhi De Jing*] says, "Kindness, charity, benevolence, and love benefit others. All assistance benefits all." If our work involves loving-kindness, compassion, joy, and equanimity, and if we take our work as a form of giving the charity of the Dharma, then we will be happy.

3) *Right behavior.* The *Ten Recitations Vinaya* [*Shi Song Lu*] states, "Hunger is the worst illness, and unwholesomeness causes the worst suffering; if one fully knows the Dharma Gem, then Nirvana will be the greatest happiness." With correct behavior, the heart will be filled with light, and there will be no afflictions or worries. This is the correct path for staying healthy.

4) *Being a good person.* The *Great Compilation of Monastic Rules* [*Mahasangha Vinaya*] teaches, "Advantage and disadvantage, praise and blame, hardship and happiness are impermanent; why be happy or sad?" The human body is composed of the four elements and, ultimately, will come to an end. Seeing through this, a person will not be subject to the five desires or six dusts, will not endeavor only for fame and self-

interest, and will not cling to the five aggregates and three realms. With the appropriate view of life, health will come naturally.

In Buddhism, mental health is viewed as important as having a healthy body. It advocates that:

1) *The mind should be free of cares and at ease.* Maitreya Bodhisattva had a tremendous capacity for forbearance. He never was calculating and was always at ease and free from obstacles.

2) *We should be calm.* The *Important Selections from the Sutras* remarks, "Being able to rid oneself of unwholesome behavior is like gaining liberation from debt, curing an illness with medicine, and leaving behind hunger for prosperity." The mind will be at ease naturally and all illnesses eliminated if we never compare or calculate, and if we are able to lift a weight and put it down.

3) *We practice meditation and cultivate the mind.* Practice vigorously and the heart will be free from worries. Everything will go smoothly, and all entanglements will vanish.

4) *We worship and never be lazy.* Worship constantly to eliminate all wrongdoings and to increase happiness.

5) *We are mindful of breathing.* We should be mindful of breathing in order to achieve the proper state of mind, stopping all delusion and seeing the truth. With the will fixed, body and mind will be focused, and we will be able to develop wisdom.

6) *Joyful progress is made by exercising the will and the mind.* Vigorous action will fulfill Dharma joys, and the body and mind will be free from illness.

Venerable Master Hanshan Deqing[52] of the Ming Dynasty said, "Who can avoid old age, sickness, death, and birth? A person must bear his/her own sourness, sweetness, bitterness, and spice. One dose of peptic powder will provide mental tranquility and a healthy stomach, while the 'double gentleness' will purge the liver of pathogenic fire." Most illnesses are linked to human psychology, physiology, behavior, and our social sur-roundings. This is especially true in this modern age. Many people eat rich food and become ill; others loaf around and get sick; some absorb too much information and end up sick; some people develop nervousness due to on-the-job stress and fall ill; others have weak dispositions and lack willpower, which makes them sick; and some argue too much and end up sick. In short, illnesses of the body and mind are caused because the mind cannot be calmed, tolerance is lacking, one cannot hold one's tongue, anger cannot be controlled, suffering cannot be borne, poverty cannot but lead to sickness, death cannot be ignored, hatred cannot be dis-pelled, self-conceit cannot be controlled, fear cannot be avoided, compe-tition cannot be curbed, arguments cannot be stopped, anxiety cannot be resolved, or wrong ideas cannot be eliminated.

To cure illness, medical science emphasizes cures involving food and drink, physics, chemistry, psychology, environment, climate, and medi-cine. Buddhism not only incorporates normal medical science but also emphasizes the elimination of the three poisons of greed, anger, and igno-rance. Diseases of the mind require medicines for the mind. Harmonizing the health of body and mind is the only way to true health. This includes the above mentioned factors: eating and drinking moder-ately, paying homage and repenting, chanting mantras and the Buddhas' names, practicing meditation, being mindful of breathing to end delu-sional thinking and see the truth, making progress optimistically, freeing the mind from cares and being at ease, and calming oneself.

On
Loving-Kindness & Compassion
the Way of Affinity

Most Buddhists are familiar with the expression, "The heart of Buddhism is loving-kindness and compassion." However, if we take the expression a step further and attempt to define the terms "loving-kindness and compassion," we will find that few are able to do so. According to *A Commentary on the Lotus Sutra*, "loving-kindness and compassion are the uprooting of suffering and the creation of joy." The Dharma methods and the teachings contained in the Buddhist Canon are infinite, but the basis for each is loving-kindness and compassion. Loving-kindness and compassion, according to the *Explanation on the Passages and Sentences of the Lotus Sutra* [*Miao Fa Lianhua Jing Wen*], are "the basis for giving charity and teaching the Dharma." Without loving-kindness and compassion, all Buddhist Dharmas would be nothing more than magic. The *Record of the Mirror of the Mind* [*Zongjing Lu*] teaches, "It is suitable to practice enlightenment with the bodhi mind as cause and loving-kindness and compassion as the basis." Bodhisattvas have compassion for all sentient beings. Compassion gives rise to bodhi, and from bodhi comes Buddhahood. Seeing the distress of sentient beings, out of loving-kindness and compassion the bodhisattva prays and transforms, uprooting suffering and giving happiness, leading sentient beings to the way of enlightenment. For this reason, loving-kindness and compassion are a prerequisite for the bodhisattva to become a Buddha.

Loving-kindness and compassion are not the exclusive property of Buddhists. They are a form of wealth possessed by all sentient beings alike. For this reason, life is filled with limitless significance. Only because of loving-kindness and compassion, there is no trepidation about one's future in this life. Loving-kindness and compassion are the eternal spring in all things; they are the Buddha Nature. With loving-kindness and compassion, all sentient beings will become Buddhas.

Loving-kindness and compassion are not synonymous with merely turning the other cheek, of not cursing when cursed. When truth and justice are pushed aside and upright persons are slandered, being able to stand up for what is right is a form of courage and an act of loving-kindness and compassion. Loving-kindness and compassion require wisdom; they are not something innate that can be felt immediately. The *Great Techniques of Stopping [Delusion] and Seeing [Truth]* states, "Wisdom is loving-kindness and compassion; loving-kindness and compassion are wisdom. We should have loving-kindness and compassion for all sentient beings and give charity without expecting anything in return. Use these qualities to uproot suffering and naturally give happiness." It is through the perception of truth that loving-kindness and compassion moves and assists people. Loving-kindness and compassion do not accompany the maddening crowd, but rather they are the true ideal that is held in the heart of helping others. Extending loving-kindness and compassion is not selfishly trying to benefit one's relatives and friends, nor is it the bestowing of charity on those who seek it. Loving-kindness and compassion represent the highest state, where all is equal, regardless of hatred or affection. They are selfless, benefiting all sentient beings.

Loving-kindness and compassion are not fixed. They are the constant elevation of feelings, or, as the *Flower Ornament Sutra* puts it: "Vowing to help all sentient beings free themselves from suffering without striving for your own happiness." This kind of "concern for the world's concerns, and happiness for the world's happiness" is loving-kindness and compassion. Loving-kindness and compassion are a prerequisite for truly being human. A person might be able to do without anything, but he/she cannot do without loving-kindness and compassion. Some people say that loving-kindness and compassion are love, but worldly love is imperfect. If not handled properly, it can immediately turn into an abyss of suffering and the source of affliction. According to *A Record of the Mysterious Significance of Avalokitesvara*, [*Guanyin Xuan Yi Ji*], "Loving-kindness and compassion are a vow." Loving-kindness and compassion are a purifying love, an elevating love. They are selflessly serving and assisting with wisdom. They are giving charity without expecting anything in return. They are a willingness to help others succeed. Loving-kindness and compassion are a gathering together of loving hearts, wisdom, willingness, and charity.

Loving-kindness and compassion are the morality of one's own deeds; they are not for the weighing of others. True loving-kindness and compassion do not necessarily have anything to do with praise and encouragement. In fact, suppressing evil with a vajra is sometimes a more difficult form of loving-kindness and compassion.

All Buddhists know about loving-kindness and compassion, everyone can talk about these terms, and some even practice them. However, some will find them difficult to understand when it comes to the deeper significance and levels of meaning. Suppose, for example, someone goes against the public good and harms others. When it comes time for sentencing, some people will ask for mercy, "Have loving-kindness and compassion; have mercy on him/her." Loving-kindness and compassion begin as general forgiveness and then become overindulgence. This is a distortion of the meaning of loving-kindness and compassion.

The Buddhist scriptures use many analogies to demonstrate the preciousness of loving-kindness and compassion. They are compared to useful medicine. When the body is diseased and suffering, medicine is needed to treat it. When the heart suffers, the Dharma water of loving-kindness and compassion are needed to soothe the afflicted mind.

Loving-kindness and compassion are like rowing a boat. On the vast sea of samsara, there is the boat of loving-kindness and compassion that can cut through the terrifying waves of fear, ferrying one to a happy and peaceful destination. It can reduce the danger of drowning in the river of cravings.

Loving-kindness and compassion are like a bright light. The shining light of loving-kindness and compassion is enough to cut through the darkness and allow one to truly see the world. With the light of loving-kindness and compassion, life has hope, and the future is something to long for. In this world of suffering, with the aid of loving-kindness and compassion, danger is smoothed away and transformed into peace.

Loving-kindness and compassion are like a friend who is always at our side encouraging us. With the friend of loving-kindness and compassion, everything is possible and will go smoothly.

Loving-kindness and compassion are like a *mani* pearl,[53] a bright pearl in dirty water. They can cleanse away impurities and help one see the bottom clearly. In this complicated, chaotic world, a *mani* pearl of loving-kindness and compassion will shine through all confusion, simplifying the complicated, turning chaos to tranquility.

Loving-kindness and compassion are the eternal spring of all things. On account of loving-kindness and compassion, people are reluctant to give up life. If a household lacks loving-kindness and compassion, it will be like an icebox, regardless of how fancy and comfortable it might be. If a service organization lacks loving-kindness and compassion, it will not attract anyone regardless of high salaries and favorable benefits. If there is no loving-kindness or compassion among relatives, then they will become like strangers and have nothing to do with one another. Why is it that Avalokitesvara is able to enter everyone's altar at home and make of everyone a worshipper? It is because Avalokitesvara represents loving-kindness and compassion. When we pay our respects to the Bodhisattva, we are hoping to bring loving-kindness and compassion into our homes.

Although loving-kindness and compassion are very important, how many people frequently misunderstand their significance? Loving-kindness and compassion begin with general forgiveness and gradually become overindulgence, affecting social order. These qualities are abused and force loving-kindness and compassion to sink into a warm bed of wrongdoing. For example, excessive charitable donations can in fact foster greed. Therefore, loving-kindness and compassion without the guidance of wisdom render them both useless. Sometimes excessive loving-kindness and compassion are given when there is no need, and other times, when loving-kindness and compassion are required, they are not given. Sometimes it does not appear to be loving-kindness or compassion, but it is; at other times what appears to be an act of loving-kindness and compassion is, in reality, not. Therefore, loving-kindness or compassion without wisdom is like a bird with one wing, or like a cart with one wheel–moving forward is out of the question, and success is impossible.

Parents who give their children money for fooling around and gambling are an example of those who bestow excessive loving-kindness and compassion when they should not. What appears to be loving-kindness and compassion is, in fact, harmful to the child. It is as if when a child does something destructive, we gladly offer encouragement by pardoning rather than punishing him/her. Such behavior is misguided loving-kindness and compassion. Another example is giving money to someone who will do unwholesome deeds and harm others. These are examples of compassionless loving-kindness.

Examples of those who should give loving-kindness and compassion but do not are those who see truth and justice being pushed aside but refuse to stand up and do anything about it. For example, some people who are able to help choose not to cooperate with and aid those who are enthusiastic about establishing schools to educate the young, but instead ruin them. This example shows a lack of loving-kindness and compassion.

Sometimes, an act that appears not to be an act of loving-kindness and compassion in fact actually is; for example, killing a murderer to save thousands of innocent people. Killing appears to lack compassion, but for the sake of thousands, it is. In helping a widow and her children, one of the three Daoist masters of the Grass Hut[54] appeared to fall victim to the five desires and lust after the woman. Actually, he was cultivating himself in the world of dust and desire. At first glance, the actions of the third disciple would not appear to be compassionate, but in fact his actions were filled with wise loving-kindness and compassion. Mallika, wife of

King Prasenajit of India, mercifully saved the King's royal chef but appeared to violate the precepts and not uphold the Dharma. Yet her actions demonstrated that she thought of others first and had a total disregard for her own life. So, in some cases, what appears not to be loving-kindness and compassion is, in fact, the loving and compassionate behavior of a bodhisattva.

Sometimes not having loving-kindness and compassion is loving-kindness and compassion; and what appears to be loving-kindness and compassion sometimes turns out not to be. For example, releasing living creatures as a deed of loving-kindness and compassion can actually be foolish behavior that results in the death of a creature. Releasing a man-eating fish at first glance might appear to be an act of loving-kindness and compassion, but once released, the fish might not only eat little fish and shrimp but also people. Is this to be considered an act of loving-kindness and compassion?

Loving-kindness and compassion involve not only rational understanding but also actual practice. When the famous Chan Master Guishan Lingyou[55] was on his deathbed, he vowed to be reborn as a water buffalo to serve and labor for others. Master Lingyou's teaching–"To be a great leader of Buddhism, one must first do service for all sentient beings"–is the mind of loving-kindness and compassion.

Master Zhishun[56] of the Tang Dynasty "split his ears to save a pheasant." To save a being from death, the Master held his own body in total disregard. The virtue of "helping to free others from their suffering without regard for one's own safety and happiness" is a concrete manifestation of loving-kindness and compassion.

Buddhist practitioners who are unwilling to harm even a blade of grass will tread carefully. They will not light a lamp at night lest a moth be drawn to the flame. For the birds that come and go, they will leave a bit of grain; so as not to step on rainy season insects, they will stay put and not travel far. All of these acts are expressions of loving-kindness and compassion.

There are also different levels of loving-kindness and compassion. Most common acts of loving-kindness and compassion performed by ordinary people, such as giving wealth and love, involve parents, spouses and children, and other relatives: those with whom we have a causal relationship. The objects of this sort of loving-kindness and compassion are limited and are generally the recipients of personal feelings of love. This is a momentary kind of loving-kindness and compassion, the loving-kindness and compassion of thoughts, causes, emotions, demands, and forms. It is passive loving-kindness and compassion.

However, for the bodhisattva, the sravaka, and the pratyeka-buddha, all dharmas are empty and arise from causes and conditions. For this reason, they help and transform, giving sentient beings what they need in accordance with conditions. This is especially true of the compassion of the Buddhas. They see themselves as identical with and equal to all sentient beings, all of which need help. This is why the loving-kindness and compassion practiced by the Buddhas and bodhisattvas is eternal, limitless, emotionless, without cause, not demanded, formless, solitary, indirect, and active. This spirit of "unconditional loving-kindness and great compassion to all as one" is actually true loving-kindness and compassion.

In this life of suffering, people depend on loving-kindness and compassion. Loving-kindness and compassion provide a ray of hope in life. Society is ruthless, tyrannical, and disorderly, and today, more than ever before, people must insist on the habits of being amiable and equitable with one another. People must learn to put themselves in the shoes of others and even to consider all sentient beings as one would him or herself. This will give rise to loving-kindness and compassion.

In China, there is a saying: "Benevolence is unmatched." In the words of Buddhism, "Loving-kindness and compassion have no equal." Loving-kindness and compassion can overcome all negativity. One thought of loving-kindness and compassion can eliminate greed, anger, arrogance, and fear. In this modern age of scientific development, it has been found that human communication is far more important than all the discoveries of science and technology. How can there be perfect communication among people? It can only happen through the practice of loving-kindness, compassion, and the four means of embracing virtue:

giving charity, using kind words, exhibiting conduct beneficial to others, and cooperating with and accommodating others to lead them to the truth. Only when people consider all sentient beings with the eyes, words, expression, voice, and mind of loving-kindness and compassion and create affinities with all sentient beings can society achieve harmony and be at peace.

On Cause & Effect

the Way of Dependent Origination

That "all people are equal before the law" is an ideal that all democracies strive to realize. But can everyone in fact be equal before the law? There are loopholes in the law; some people exist on the margins of the law where they do evil; and sometimes the law is bent unjustly. For these reasons, the law is not absolutely fair. In this world, only cause and effect are absolutely fair and impartial. Before the Law of Cause and Effect, everyone is equal. Cause and effect and karmic retribution are as inseparable as shape and shadow. No one can escape from the implacable Law of Cause and Effect in which "good is rewarded with good, and evil with evil."

"Reaping what one sows" is the simplest way to explain cause and effect. This is the universal principle for all arising, extinction, and change. The *Commentary on the Stages of Yogacara Practitioners* [*Yogacarabhumi Sastra*] states, "What is done cannot be undone; what is not done will accomplish nothing." These words elaborate on the special characteristics of the Buddhist concept of cause and effect. All thoughts and actions will result in corresponding effects. A "cause" produces an "effect"; it will not vanish of its own accord. By the same token, if no deed is committed to produce a cause, then no corresponding effect will be produced.

The Law of Cause and Effect is a reality of life. China's *Twenty-Six Books of History*[57] comprise the largest, most detailed, accurate, and profound record of cause and effect. The Law of Cause and Effect is a profound philosophy. For every cause there must be an effect. Its accuracy is far beyond that of modern computer technology. Cause and effect and karmic retribution are beyond human coercion; heaven cannot change them, and even ghosts and spirits cannot oppose them. They govern everything in human life and extend through the three lives of the past, present, and future. The *Nirvana Sutra* cautions, "Good and bad karma are like the shadow that follows a shape. The cycle of cause and effect never vanishes from life to life. Once this life is gone and accomplishments are none, it is too late for regrets." This being the case, a person should not fear ghosts and spirits or birth and death, but they must fear karmic retribution and cause and effect.

Cause and effect are controlled and instigated by the force and seeds of causes. The Law of Cause and Effect operates independently. Human beings can change the will of heaven but not its rational order, which is to say the Law of Cause and Effect cannot be changed. Cause, as contrasted with effect, is the truth of nature realized by the Buddha and the inviolable dharma realms known to all Buddhas of the past, present, and future.

The Buddhist concept of cause and effect originates in the principles of dependent origination and emptiness. To clarify: all things and events in the universe depend upon "causes" being consigned to "conditions" to produce "effects." These "effects" in turn become "causes" until "conditions" accumulate, producing their "effects." This occurs again and again in a cycle, producing all things. Thus, nothing in the universe, from the world of nature to the world of sentient beings, from celestial body and mote of dust, can escape from the Law of Cause and Effect. The expression, "Dharmas do not arise alone and need objects to be produced; the Way does not operate in vain and when conditions accumulate, dharmas arise" means that for anything there must be causes and conditions before there can be effects. We must be aware that cause and effect cannot be isolated from dependent origination.

The Law of Cause and Effect is not a special truth limited to the purview of Buddhism. The Law of Cause and Effect is found in the dressing, eating, dwelling, and walking of each and every person. Reach out and you can touch it; it is a truth, the proof of which is everywhere at hand. When you are hungry, you eat. Eating is the "cause," and a full stomach is the "effect." First there must be the "cause" of an empty stomach before there can be the "effect" of a full stomach. When it gets cold, we must wear more clothing to stay warm. Cold is the "cause," and warmth is the "effect." Even the wearing of clothing is inseparable from the Law of Cause and Effect.

Not only are there causes and effects for dressing, eating, dwelling, and walking, but also for happiness and disaster as well as birth and death. The number of good deeds we cultivated in the past is directly related to our blessed rewards in the present. Nowhere in the world is there an effect without a cause, nor is there a cause without an effect. There is neither effect without its corresponding cause, nor a cause without its corresponding effect. As such, cause and effect are determined by one's own actions and behavior.

The Law of Cause and Effect extends through the past, present, and future and covers the ten directions. Cause and effect exist whether we believe in them or not. Like air, they pervade the universe and at all times fairly mete out good and evil, rewards and punishments to all sentient beings, as well as the success and failure of the world. For example, some people are born to live in mansions or in high-rises and are never troubled by extreme heat or cold, while others live in slums and shanties, exposed to the elements. This is not because the world is unfair, but due to differences in cause and condition and karmic retribution. Although all are born as human beings, why are some wealthy and some poor? Why do some dress well and eat like kings while others go hungry without three meals a day? This is because of the differences in the causes they have sown and the effects they reap, and is not due to fate or the unfairness of the world. Cultivating a certain causal ground will lead to a certain kind of retribution. Cause and effect are complementary. Invariably, creating a certain kind of karma will result in a certain kind of retribution.

Cause and effect are equivalent to "cause and condition, effect and retribution." Cause is primary and condition is secondary. Together they produce effects. In the universe, objects as large as planets or as small as specks of dust have no real existence of their own to speak of. However, because causes and conditions vary, so do effects. According to Buddhist teachings, the relationship between life and the Law of Cause and Effect is a very close one. The Buddhist Law of Cause and Effect is a fact of life in the cosmos and not just something said to encourage good behavior. But most people explain cause and effect in a mundane way. Unfortunately, people who do not understand Buddhism misinterpret this as some sort of superstition. For a correct understanding of cause and effect, there are several things we should keep in mind:

1) *Cause and effect pervade time past, present, and future.* According to the *Record of the Mirror of the Mind*, "A gatha reads, 'Even after millions of kalpas, karma remains; when causes and conditions ripen, retribution will be effected.'" Although the relationship between cause and effect and karmic retribution is a complex one, it is systematic and unerring. Some people do not understand the Law of Cause and Effect. They only see that a good person suffers and dies young, and a bad person enjoys a wealthy, comfortable life; for this reason, they assume that the Law of Cause and Effect does not exist. In fact, cause and effect pervade the past, present, and future, and we cannot determine their existence based on one moment in time. The law is simple. For example, if someone saved a lot of money in the bank in the past and now breaks the law, can the person be prohibited from drawing on his/her savings? If a person had a lot of debt in the past and is now practicing good, the debts must still be repaid. Can you say that just because this person is cultivating good now, he/she need not return the money?

Thus, a good person might suffer in this life because the evil causes planted in the past are now ripe. Although one practices good in this life, because the good causes are weak and not yet ripe, one will experience good only in a future life. The same principle applies to a bad person who lives comfortably in this life.

Next, cause and effect and karmic retribution exist in three time periods: past, present, and future. Take plants as an example. There are annuals, biennials, and perennials. The seeds of some are sown in spring and harvested in the fall; the seeds of others are sown this year and harvested next year; and some seeds are sown this year but not harvested until many years later. Cause and effect and karmic retribution are as inseparable as form and shadow. In creating positive or negative causes, it does not matter whether time is long or short; once the causes ripen, there will be retribution. Of this there is no doubt.

2) *The Law of Cause and Effect is not the same as fatalism.* Fatalism holds that gain and loss, success and failure, are all determined by the hand of fate and that any effort on one's part to change it is useless. But the Buddhist Law of Cause and Effect holds that retribution, both positive and negative, is created by the individual. A gatha describes this situation: "Having food and clothing is the result of what causes? By having provided the poor with food and drink in past lives. Not having food and clothing is the result of what causes? By not having provided half a cent to charity. Having fine clothes to wear is the result of what causes? By having provided monastics with robes in past lives. Having a noble visage is the result of what causes? By having offered food and flowers to the Buddhas in past lives."

The *Ten Verses on Cause and Effect* says:

> Uprightness comes from enduring humiliation;
>> poverty comes from greed.
> High position comes from paying respect and homage;
>> low position comes from pride.
> Muteness comes from slander;
>> blindness and deafness come from lack of faith.
> Longevity comes from compassion;
>> early death comes from acts of killing.

This verse shows that poverty and wealth, rank, life span, and even physical features are the result of an individual's past karma, good and bad, and not determined by someone else, much less fate. Therefore, the Law of Cause and Effect affirms individual effort and progress. It is an optimistic law that encourages us to keep forging ahead.

3) *Everything is due to cause and effect.* In the formation of all worldly dharmas, "cause" is that which gives rise, while "effect" is that which arises. The simplest and most easily understood explanation of the relationship between cause and effect is the expression, "One will reap what one sows." If you plant melons, you harvest melons; and if you plant beans, you harvest beans. Plants are this way as is everything else. Thus, "Good produces good karma, and bad produces bad karma. It is not that there is no karma but that the time is not ripe." Furthermore, the workings of cause and effect transcend ordinary social consensus and the limitations of the law. For this reason, Dr. Sun Yat-sen said, "The benevolence of Buddhism is in saving the world; the Dharma can compensate for deficiencies in the law."

The Law of Cause and Effect is much more than a field of theoretical study. Everything in our daily lives–dressing, eating, dwelling, walking, as well as the way we deal with each other, faith, morality, health, and economics–is related to the Law of Cause and Effect. However, some people do not properly understand this law, and for this reason, in their faith they make many unreasonable demands. For instance, they become vegetarians for health reasons, or they worship the Buddha to obtain high position and wealth. These are erroneous views of the Law of Cause and Effect. Actually, when it comes to faith, the Law of Cause and Effect is also involved with morality, health, and wealth. Therefore, if people want to be healthy, they must control their emotions, exercise, and be conscious of their well-being. With a calm mind, their bodies will be at ease. If people want to increase their wealth, they must form more good ties, work diligently and with patience, stand by their word and fulfill promises, and be intelligent and hard working. Heaven helps those who help themselves.

Vegetarianism and worshipping the Buddha are causes and effects related to faith and morality. If the cause of faith is used to pursue the effects of health and wealth, or if causes and effects are mixed erroneously, there will be no way to achieve what is desired. This is the necessity of cause and effect.

4) *An individual creates the retribution he/she receives.* According to the *Sutra of the Past Vows of the Earth Store Bodhisattva*, "Do not assume that because a wrongdoing is small it is not a crime; retribution may not end even after death. Though father and son are related, their paths divide; though they meet, one does not pay for the wrongdoings of the other." These words clearly demonstrate that "causes, good and bad, determine the karma" and that "each individual creates the karmic retribution he/she receives."

Power and influence cannot influence the Law of Cause and Effect and karmic retribution. Ghosts and spirits cannot affect them; heaven cannot control them; they are part and parcel of life. They are the measure and basis of our behavior, good and bad. The Law of Cause and Effect is not a religious commandment. It is a universal ruler in everyone's heart for measuring one's fate and good and bad. It is also a way to create a future self. For this reason, we should take seriously the principles of cause and effect. By planting good causes in this life, we will be able to bring wisdom and happiness to this life and future lives.

Generally speaking, etiquette, morals, and the law bind a society together. But the greatest force is the Law of Cause and Effect. The restraints imposed by the law are tangible, and there are limits to the control exercised by etiquette and morals. Nothing can compare with the severity and directness of the idea of cause and effect, when it is harbored deep in the minds of people.

The Law of Cause and Effect is not just a penetrating concept; it is an affirmation of our behavior. Those who practice the Way often criticize contemporary society, saying that it is "cut off from the past and degenerating day by day." Why are such things said? It is because people these days lack any concept of the Law of Cause and Effect. And because people do not understand the Law of Cause and Effect, they do not fear it. They cheat, covet, steal, and take advantage of others whenever they can. In any case, worldly law is not perfect, and when someone breaks the law, it might go unknown. Even if someone knows a crime has been committed, it does not mean that the law will be upheld. While the law may not be upheld in society, the Law of Cause and Effect is implacable.

If a person does something immoral, he/she might well escape worldly law, but not the judgment of a good conscience and the Law of Cause and Effect. After a Japanese minister died, five words were found in his clothes: falsehood, reason, law, power, and heaven. The significance of the five words is: "falsehood" cannot overcome "reason"; "reason" cannot overcome "law"; "law" cannot overcome "power"; and "power" cannot overcome "heaven." "Heaven" is nothing but the Law of Cause and Effect. It is the ultimate victor.

When the Buddha himself lived in this world, he was like the rest of us, subject to birth, old age, sickness, death, and the Law of Cause and Effect. Great indeed is this idea, for it means everyone is equal before the Law of Cause and Effect. Nobody can escape it.

Life as we know it is without beginning or end. Karma manifests itself throughout people's lives, over time, into the past, present, and future. By examining past, present, and future, we will find that what we experience today, the poverty and wealth and the gain and loss, are directly related to the Law of Cause and Effect. The causes one plants at a moment in one's life can influence an entire life or the fortune and disaster of future lives. This being the case, how can one not carefully consider his/her speech and actions, even for a moment? For our life's sake as well as for the sake of coming lives, we must pay attention to the causes and effects of each moment.

The scriptures tell us that, "Bodhisattvas fear causes while sentient beings fear effects." The Law of Cause and Effect functions as one's own policeman and teacher; it is one's own legal norm. In the expression, "If a person is kind, others may take advantage of him/her, but heaven does not; if a person is bad, others may be afraid of him, but heaven is not." Heaven is the same as the Law of Cause and Effect. It is just. Since we advocate Humanistic Buddhism, a sound understanding of the Law of Cause and Effect–past, present, and future–will enable us to forsake evil and practice good, incline toward happiness and avoid suffering, and even if we should be subject to bad karma in this life, we will not complain to heaven and fault others, but bear it with a sense of personal responsibility, transforming bad causes into good.

This is especially the case when the Law of Cause and Effect is considered over the past, present, and future. Knowing that sentient beings are subject to the way of karma and are reborn will allow us to care for each other as if we were family. Such awareness will stimulate us to practice "unconditional loving-kindness and great compassion to all as one." Not only will we find satisfaction in this life, but even more so in future lives. Therefore, a clear understanding of the Law of Cause and Effect and karmic retribution will allow one to take hold of karma in the search for one's own happiness.

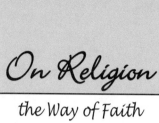

On Religion

the Way of Faith

Humans are religious beings. Religion is like light and water, neither of which humans can live without. In the remote past, when humans were still uncivilized, they already possessed faith in nature. This was followed by the development of theocracy and monarchy, the democracy and human rights of today, and the rights of all living things in the future. From the beginnings of human civilization, humanity has constantly sought not only to live a satisfying material life but also to promote a spiritual life of faith.

Faith is natural, an inherent spiritual force. However, faith does not necessarily mean faith in a religion. For example, some people have faith in a particular idea or theory; some people have faith in a particular 'ism'; while some people worship a person to the extent that it becomes a faith.

This may be so, but once the questions of life and death are posed, then faith in a religion is certainly involved. Faith in a religion requires careful choices. For once a person believes in the false beliefs of a cult, it is no different from a person drinking poison. Once the poison takes hold, his or her life is at risk. It is therefore better to have no beliefs at all rather than to have evil beliefs. And having superstitious beliefs is better than having no beliefs, because although superstition stems from not fully understanding the truth, there is some concept of good and evil and cause and effect. The tendency is to do good and shun evil. A person without faith or beliefs is like a person who does not think or who refuses to open his/her eyes and look at the world. Never will he/she have the opportunity to understand this world.

The ultimate form of faith is, of course, correct faith. A religion of correct faith requires certain things:

1) *A faith must have historical basis.* In the case of Sakyamuni Buddha of Buddhism, there are historical records of his parents, his clan, his place and date of birth, and his process of leaving home, cultivation, and enlightenment.

2) *A faith must be widely acknowledged.* Buddhism, for instance, is recognized as one of the world's four great religions.

3) *There must be faith in human dignity, morality, and perfection.* The Buddha, for example, possesses the three complete virtues of wisdom, freedom from ignorance, and universal grace. He is the perfectly enlightened practitioner of merit.

4) *The power of faith must be awe-inspiring and complete.* For example, the three Dharma seals, the Four Noble Truths, and the Noble Eightfold Path, as well as the Laws of Cause and Effect, karma, and dependent origination of Buddhism are all irrefutable truths. They can help lead us to the truth and forsake suffering for happiness.

Faith is the ultimate goal. It can support us in life. Regardless of which religion a person believes in, a rational choice must be made based on whether the teachings of the religion are in accord with the truth. That is to say that a religion must be universal, equal, real, and eternal. For example, the Buddhist scriptures speak of "four unattainables": perpetual youth, no sickness, perennial life, and no death (*Sutra on the Four Unattainables Discoursed by the Buddha* [*Fo Shuo Si Bukede Jing*]). This is a universal truth for the Chinese as well as men or women from other countries. It was as true in history as it is today and as it will be in the future. It is a universal, real, original, and eternal truth.

Buddhism is a religion that accords with the truth. If we examine the histories, ancient and modern, we read about how Emperor Wu of the

Liang Dynasty[58] forsook Daoism[59] for Buddhism, how King Asoka made Buddhism the national religion, and how Lu Mengzheng,[60] the famous minister of the Song Dynasty said, "I pray that those who do not have faith in the Triple Gem will not be born in my household. I pray that my descendents all can work for the court and protect the Buddhist faith abroad." Nietzsche, the philosopher and son of a minister, praised Buddhism as being truer and more sublime than Christianity. Schopenhauer considered himself a Buddhist, affirming that Buddhism was the world's most honorable religion. Han Yu,[61] who once opposed worshipping Buddhist relics, converted to Buddhism. Ouyang Xiu[62] went from slandering the Dharma to practicing Buddhism. Even Asvaghosa, Nagarjuna, Aryadeva, Asanga, and Vasubandhu, five great Buddhist commentators, all converted to Buddhism from other religions.

There are different levels of faith in Buddhism. For example, some people "believe in a person and not in the Dharma"; some people "believe in a temple but not in a religion"; some people "believe in a feeling and not in the Way"; and some people "believe in spirits but not in the Buddhas."

There are even differences in the faith within Buddhist teachings. For most people, prajna is synonymous with correct views. For those of the two vehicles, prajna is dependent origination. For the bodhisattva, prajna is emptiness. Only the Buddha is capable of true awareness of prajna. Prajna is the realm of the Buddhas, the supreme dharma realm of one reality.

Due to the different capacities among sentient beings, the Dharma is divided into five methods of spiritual practice, also known as the "five vehicles." Buddhism for humans and devas emphasizes improving one's mind by actively doing good in this life to achieve happiness in this life and the next. For Buddhism, this is the law of the world. On the level of humans, it bears similarities to Confucianism and on the level of devas, to Christianity and Islam. Buddhism for sravakas and pratyeka-buddhas emphasizes a detached mind for liberation and leaving the world. Its ultimate goal is happiness by achieving liberation through nirvana. It is similar to Daoism in renouncing the world, being free of desires, and seeking nature and calmness. Buddhism for bodhisattvas emphasizes the bodhi-mind of benefiting the world. The ultimate goal is to cultivate the supreme happiness of compassion and wisdom and to liberate all sentient beings through the practice of the six perfections and all modes of liberation.

The teachings of Buddhism are profound and all encompassing. In addition to taking refuge in the Triple Gem advocated by Buddhism, Buddhists can pay respect to the gods. Taking refuge and worshipping are different; taking refuge is faith for a lifetime, while worship is a moment of respect. Therefore, Buddhists who have taken refuge in the Triple Gem can worship various deities. But faith presupposes a single and focused mind. Hence, we read in the "Universal Gateway" chapter of the *Lotus Sutra*, "single-mindedly recite the bodhisattva's name" and "single-mindedly make offerings." In the *Amitabha Sutra*, we read: "single-minded and undisturbed" and "single-mindedly wish to be reborn in the Pure Land." These quotations stand as proof of the importance of whole-heartedness and sincerity of spirit. Thus, adherents of a particular religion must be loyal to their chosen faith. They must be focused, for when their faith conflicts with their feelings, money, occupation, or future, they must be able to single-mindedly confront the test.

It does not matter in what religion a person believes. The most important thing is to uncover one's original nature, or what is meant by the expression, "Depend upon oneself and the Dharma and nothing else" (*Treatise on the Perfection of Great Wisdom*). Those who possess correct faith not only have spiritual and mental support, they also can broadly form good affinities with like-minded friends. As the *Buddhist Canon of the Theravada Tradition* asserts, "In a household that has faith, there are four types of morality: there is sincerity, truth, firmness, and giving charity in life." With these four types of morality, there will be "no fear or anxieties with regard to the present or the future." If a person has no fear or anxiety with regard to life and death, then he/she already possesses correct faith as far as Buddhism is concerned. As the *Diamond Sutra* notes, "If a person can produce even one thought of pure faith, he/she will achieve anuttarasamyaksambodhi."

In conclusion, religious faith can inspire us with the courage and strength to face the future. It can provide us with the magnanimity to forgive the unfairness of life and thereby create an entirely new fate. The teachings of Buddhism, especially the Middle Way and dependent origination, the Law of Cause and Effect and karmic retribution, and nirvana can all help us solve the riddle of life, revealing the original Buddha Nature of all people. Thus, to believe in Buddhism, one must progress from beseeching, believing in, and worshipping the Buddha to studying Buddhism and doing as the Buddha did to become a Buddha, which is the highest faith of all.

On Life

the Way of Birth and Death

The human life span is short, no more than several decades. With birth, there must be death. Birth and death are events that every person must face.

Birth and death follow one upon the other much like a shadow follows a body. Birth entails death, and death leads to rebirth; birth and death, over and over, without end. Where do we come from at birth, and where do we go after death? Most people do not know. The Buddhist concept of the twelve links of dependent origination holds that sentient beings accumulate "ignorance," which creates "mental formation," which in turn produces "consciousness." The "alaya consciousness" gradually develops into a living being in the mother's womb, which is referred to as "mind and form." "Mind" is the spiritual part of a living being, while "form" refers to the actual physical body. After several months, the "six sense organs"–eyes, ears, nose, tongue, body, and mind–develop. After birth, the infant comes into "contact" with its outer surroundings. It begins to have "feelings" of happiness and sadness, which produce "cravings" and lead to "grasping." As a result of the behavior of body, speech, and mind, the seeds of "becoming" of future lives are planted. With birth, it is impossible to avoid old age and death. "Death" represents the beginning of yet another life. Therefore, Buddhism holds that the cycle of life is "transmigration," without beginning or end.

Believing in Buddhism does not mean that one can avoid confronting the issues of birth and death. The focus is on breaking the cycle of birth and death, or samsara. Samsara is natural. Even the Buddhas "appear in the world when causes and conditions are ripe; when causes and conditions cease, Buddhas enter parinirvana; they come and go for all sentient beings."

The Buddhist scriptures divide death into four main types: 1) death due to age, 2) death due to the exhaustion of blessings, 3) death due to accidents, and 4) death beyond the cycle of birth and death. Death is neither extinction nor slumber. It is not like the dispersal of ashes and smoke, nor is it without feelings or consciousness. It is an exit from one world and an entrance to another, the transmigration from one world into another. Through death, people may ascend to a bright spiritual world. It is for this reason that many positive metaphors are applied to death in the Buddhist scriptures. For example:

1) *Death is like release from jail.* According to the *Treatise on the Perfection of Great Wisdom*, "The sufferings are like hell." Bodily existence and the suffering of so many afflictions can be likened to being imprisoned. Death is like being freed from jail. One will be free and no longer subject to any restraints.

2) *Death is like being reborn.* Death is a new beginning, not an end. The *Sutra Requested by Visesacinta Brahma Deva* [*Visesacintabrahmapariprccha Sutra*] remarks, "It is like oil being extracted from sesame seeds or butter being churned from milk."

3) *Death is like graduation.* The *Great Nirvana Sutra* [*Parinirvana Sutra*] states, "The teachings passed down eliminate all sorts of ignorance, making a success of study." Life is analogous to going to school, and death is graduation. One's grades and performance in the past influence one's rebirth.

4) *Death is like moving.* Every living thing is subject to death. Death is nothing more than moving the body out of this

broken-down, old, and corrupt house and returning to one's profound and pervasive spiritual home. As the *Sutra of Illuminating Light* describes it, "The deer returns to the wild and the bird to the skies; doctrines are realized and the enlightened enters nirvana."

5) *Death is like changing clothes.* Death is like removing old worn-out garments and putting on new ones. As the *Lankavatara Sutra* tells us, "Even as vast as the world of ten directions is, in the mind of the Tathagata, it is no more than a small cloud in the boundless sky." Life in this world of dust and all its experiences are like clouds passing before the eyes. It all amounts to nothing more than a garment.

6) *Death is like the new replacing the old.* The new is always replacing the old in our bodies. Only after old cells die do new ones replace them. The *Gradual Discourses of the Buddha* states, "Superseding makes change easy; there is no end or dissolution." Samsara is like new cells replacing old ones. The fact that the old is always being replaced by the new makes life all the more precious.

Buddhism often calls death "rebirth"; it is like going on a trip or moving. This being the case, is not death also a joyful event? Therefore, death is a transformational stage, when one life is reborn in another life. For this reason, death is not something to be feared. One must be calm in the face of death and let nature take its course.

People fear death because life can be conceptualized, but death cannot. That is why the end of life seems so sad. Actually, life is like water in a cup. When the cup is broken, it is broken. The water runs over the table and onto the ground, but it can be sponged up and put into another cup. Although the cup is broken, the water of life is not diminished by as much as even one drop.

"Nirvana is equanimity" is an apt expression. There is no birth or death; nothing arises nor is anything extinguished. True life transcends the impermanent and the non-self. This is analogous to the surging of waves in the sea. Is the foam on the water's surface seawater or a wave? From an enlightened perspective, the wind raises the waves. Without wind, the sea is smooth. The greatest chaos always returns to quietude. This resembles the analogy above: a cup might be broken and irreparable, but the water remains. A further comparison to fire can be made. As long as firewood is added to a fire, the flames will not go out. By the same token, life itself never ends.

"Life does not end" because of karma. Karma is the actions of body, speech, and mind. There is positive karma, negative karma, and neutral karma. "Even after eons, karma is not extinguished." Good karma or otherwise need only be created by body, speech, and mind, and it will function like a computer, where karma is stored in the memory. "When causes and conditions ripen, retribution will be affected" (*Record of the Mirror of Mind*). When the causes of karma ripen, everything will happen of its own accord. This reaping as one sows is the inescapable law of karma.

Scientists today say that the code of life is the gene. Actually, the code of life is karma–another name for the gene. The Buddha taught humanity this 2,500 years ago. "Karma" is the Buddha's great discovery. Human life extends from the remote past to today and will extend into the future because karma resembles a thread, stringing all the countless births and deaths together in one unbroken continuum that cannot be dispersed nor diminished in the slightest. Karma determines a person's place of birth. Therefore, if a person "wishes to know the causes of a previous life, all he/she needs to do is look at the retribution in this life. If a person wants to know the effects in a future life, all he/she needs to do is examine his/her deeds in this life." Therefore, "doing good and not bad" is a form of genetic engineering.

Karma determines the life and death of all sentient beings. Liberated sages use their own wills to fulfill their lives. The cycle of birth and death is a natural principle. Just as Chan Master Zongle observed, "The life and death of a human being is like foam on the sea, appearing and disappearing and returning to the water." Perhaps Chan Master Daokai[63] put it even better when he taught: "I am seventy-six and my time is nearly up. In life I did not love heaven, in death I will not fear hell. Scatter me beyond the three realms and what is to prevent me from soaring where I will?" In dying, some Chan masters first made offerings before dying; some died while sitting or standing; some sang as they drowned; and some climbed mountains and dug their own graves. All were carefree beyond compare.

In Buddhism, there are many instances when a person who foretold his/her final moments did not suffer from disease. This shows that there is nothing strange in mastering birth and death. What we really want to transcend is the conceptualizations of birth and death. The Chan School holds that, "Eliminating the fear of birth and death allows a person to accomplish anything and the Dharma-body to live." The short time in which our consciousness is arising, extinguishing, and changing is described in the *Sutra on Transmigrating in the Realms of Existence* [*Dasheng Liuzhuan Zhu You Jing*] as, "The extinguishing of consciousness is a kind of death; the arising of thoughts is life." At each moment we are facing life and death. The birth and death of consciousness and the arising and extinguishing of thoughts are like a cataract. The only way to cut the flow of samsara is not to become attached to any thoughts or ideas. If one can experience dependent origination and the essential emptiness of all things, it would be like arriving at an awareness of the oneness of birth and death, at a state beyond birth and death. "If one can be as impassive as a wooden bird and look at nature, then regardless of whatever is around you, you will not be affected." That is why the scriptures teach, "When thought is extinguished, it goes nowhere; when thought arises, it comes from nowhere."

Life does not start after birth, nor does it end with death. If life were so simple, then birth and death would not be things to fear. Chan Master Daoyuan[64] said, "Liberation from the cycle of birth and death is a great Buddhist purpose." He also said, "If the Buddha exists in our minds, then samsara can be transcended. Understanding samsara is the basis of nirvana. Having transcended samsara, birth and death will not be loathed, nor will nirvana be something sought after. That is why this is referred to as a great purpose." If we can clearly understand this principle, eliminate all confusion, and verify the Truth, then we will realize that birth and death are the same as nirvana, and we will not be confused by birth and death. We will be able to dwell peacefully beyond birth and death. This being the case, why should we hold onto fears about death.

Death is not worth fearing. Death is like immigration. You can go to another country, and as long as you have sufficient means and the merit to accrue wealth, then why fear the inability to survive? Therefore, death is not necessarily that frightening. Where one goes after death is the most important thing.

Buddhism takes the issue of life and death very seriously. In fact, Buddhism is the study of life and death. For example, Avalokitesvara Bodhisattva's goal to "liberate sentient beings from suffering and hardship" is a way of solving the question of life. Amitabha Buddha's "welcome to the Pure Land" is a way of solving the question of death. The ultimate aim of those who study Buddhism is to attain liberation from life and death. How to firmly grasp the present life and free oneself from samsara have always been central issues for Buddhists.

In life, some people understand nothing but eating, drinking, and making merry or struggling for fame and personal gain. They are as lacking in consciousness as a walking corpse. They have no idea of what to seek for themselves in life or how to prepare for the hereafter. They just muddle along one day at a time. When death comes, everything will have been for naught. One must first understand how to live before one understands how to die. The Dharma seeks to make us familiar with life and death. We need to change the old negative mindsets that make us avoid talking about taboo subjects such as life and death. Then we should adopt the correct attitude toward life and death by practicing and upholding the Dharma. Our lives will truly be happy only if we can deal with and attain liberation from life and death.

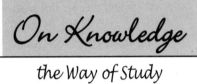

On Knowledge

the Way of Study

Study can increase knowledge and bring wisdom as well as improve one's disposition, perfect one's character, and alter one's temperament. This is why it is said that, "by knowing the classics one glorifies oneself." People who do not study are unrefined and their words lack luster. Put a person who studies side by side with one who does not. Although they are alike in that both have parents and both wear clothes and eat, they are as different as night and day when it comes to their moral character and temperament. This is why since ancient times wise people have encouraged everyone to study.

Buddhism is a religion of wisdom and faith. Its aim is to enlighten sentient beings as well as eliminate their afflictions and sufferings. This is why Buddhism places emphasis on the "life of a scholar," encouraging all Buddhists to read the scriptures and listen to the Dharma. For instance, the *Father and Son Sutra* [*Fuzi Heji Jing*] teaches, "If sentient beings hear the Buddha's words, their hearts will give rise to pure faith and a resolve to attain liberation; by single-mindedly practicing the wonderful way, they will attain perfect wisdom, transcending the sea of samsara." The *Lankavatara Sutra* notes, "By first hearing and contemplating, then practicing, one attains samadhi." This is why all Buddhist sutras begin with the words, "Thus have I heard." A gatha states, "The incomparably profound and wonderful Dharma is difficult to encounter in countless kalpas. Today, I hear, receive, and uphold it to attain the Buddha's perfect wisdom." The *Diamond Sutra* states, "The merit from receiving and upholding but four lines of this gatha is superior to all the offerings of wealth in countless worlds." And the *Flower Ornament Sutra* affirms, "Of all offerings, an offering of the Dharma is best." All these examples recommend a life of study.

Buddhism emphasizes wisdom. The ancient temples and monasteries in China served as schools where monastics could study and practice the Way. Hence the expression, "Among so many monastics who have traveled far and studied to a great extent, is there an enlightened one to be found?" Even in more recent times, many elders at the end of the Qing Dynasty[65] and beginning of the Republic of China established monastic and secular schools; in particular, Master Taixu[66] established many Buddhist academies. Today in Taiwan, there are Sunday schools and summer camps for children; there are youth groups and college groups for young people; there are practice and study groups for devotees; and there are even Buddhist institutes and graduate schools for professionals. The kindergartens, primary schools, middle schools, and high schools as well as the universities established by Fo Guang Shan have all received the support of millions of devotees. These examples serve to clearly demonstrate that all Buddhists realize the importance of education and knowledge.

Buddhism is the teachings of the Buddha. Temples are places to study and practice Buddhism; therefore, in ancient times, they were called "the venue for selecting the Buddha." Temples were schools, and Buddhism placed a premium on the transmission of written wisdom. The "ten Dharma practices" of the *Lotus Sutra* included the benefits of writing, speaking, reading, and printing the sutras. The *Amitabha Sutra* states that at every hour of every day, beings who reside in the Pure Land think about the Buddha, the Dharma, and the Sangha. At every moment they seek to benefit all beings by being mindful of the Buddha and the Dharma. The "Entering the Dharma Realm" chapter of the *Flower Ornament Sutra* tells how young Sudhana sets his mind on seeking the

Dharma and goes through the arduous process of traveling to visit fifty-three good Dharma friends in the search for knowledge. This is similar to the study abroad programs of today and serves as a model for today's youth as they venture forth to study.

Yuan Liaofan[67] of the Ming Dynasty said, "The spoken word is sufficient to persuade others for a moment, but books for a hundred years. To do good is the happiest thing; the merit is all encompassing. The five precepts can guarantee that one is reborn in the human realm; the ten wholesome conducts lead to rebirth in the heavenly realm. The Law of Cause and Effect does not set everything in stone, and study is of benefit." From ancient times, Buddhism has placed a premium on the wisdom contained in the written word. Almost every temple contained a building in which the scriptures were kept. In addition to the ten thousand words chanted daily, there exist handwritten pattra-leaf[68] sutras as well as those carved in stone. Then there is the example of Bhiksuni Fazhen,[69] who lost an arm printing sutras during the Yuan Dynasty. There are also the examples of Venerable Master Xuanzang, who collected sutras in India and the western regions of China, and Dharmodgata, who spread the Dharma to the East. They sought out and propagated the Dharma, without thinking of themselves. If they had not studied, would this have been possible? Without the scholarly life, would we possess the Buddhist Canon today?

In addition, Tang Dynasty Chan Master Guishan Lingyou remarked, "Speech involves rules and one should hew to the ancient ways. One's bearing should be upright; one's spirit lofty and relaxed." Venerable Master Ouyi said, "Immoderation in food and drink will produce illness; not reading the Buddhist Canon will keep the eye of wisdom shut." Venerable Master Zhuhong[70] of the Ming Dynasty advocated, "Everyone in this world has something they like, and this they pursue all the days of their lives. The pure and impure differ. The most impure crave wealth, sex, and wine. Better are those who like antiques, music, chess, or scenery and poetic recitation. The best are those who like to study. They benefit from reading. Of all the things people enjoy, study is the best. Even better is studying the Buddhist sutras and purifying one's mind. The purity of the mind is the greatest in worldly and transcendental living. Gradually entering this perfect state is like eating sugarcane." From these examples, it is clear that the moral exemplars of antiquity emphasized study, especially the earnest study of the scriptures.

From ancient times, all those who have become monastics have been widely read in the scriptures. Naturally, most of them such as Su Dongpo[71] and Chan Master Foyin,[72] Bai Juyi[73] and Chan Master Niaoke, Ouyang Xiu and Chan Master Mingjiao,[74] and Yuan Liaofan and Chan Master Yungu Hui,[75] were intellectuals and had close connections with the scholarly class. Even Han Yu, the avowed opponent of Buddhism, was a friend of and sought instruction from Chan Master Dadian.[76] In traditional China, male and female villagers who could not recite the Confucian classics could recite Buddhist texts such as the *Great Compassion Dharani*, the *Diamond Sutra*, and the *Amitabha Sutra*. Clearly, the Buddhist advocacy for education has always pervaded society.

According to the *Sutra on the Contemplation of the Mind*, "First become friends with good Dharma friends; second, listen to the true Dharma; third, contemplate the truth; and fourth, practice the Way." The *Vigilance for All Monastics [Zimen Jingxun]* asserts, "Nothing is possible without study. Nothing can be learned without humbling oneself; the Dharma cannot be held without a teacher; nothing will be remembered without practice and recitation." Buddhism stresses the transmission of knowledge and the cultivation of wisdom. However, Buddhist education differs from ordinary education that seeks to develop skills that can be used to earn a living or a diploma with which to obtain a good job. Buddhist education includes compassion, a shouldering of the great burden to benefit oneself and others.

Buddhist education can be roughly divided into two categories: temple administration and theoretical research with special emphasis on education for life and thought. Life education includes training in walking, dwelling, sitting, resting, communicating with others, and behavior. Thought education means first of all to possess the four objects of unfailing faith: 1) faith in the Triple Gem; 2) faith in the temple; 3) compassion for all sentient beings; and 4) firmness in upholding the precepts.

Studying must be self-motivated and spontaneous, and one must take the initiative. Buddhism, unlike most philosophies, does not just speak of knowledge, theory, and ethics, but emphasizes practice and cultivation. The saying "understanding and practicing are of equal importance" means that one must not merely have a deep understanding and knowledge of the Dharma, but one must practice it in life. In this way, cultivation is something to be practiced in life and not just an empty slogan or form. For example, one should use words of compassion to reply to others, look at others with compassionate eyes, present a compassionate appearance to others, assist others with hands of compassion, and bless others with a compassionate heart. Only when life is imbued with the Dharma can it be called practice.

The *Lankavatara Sutra* states, "If one hears the Dharma but fails to practice it, it is the same as never having heard it. This is like a person who can 'eat' but never gets full by doing so." The study and practice of Buddhism are not limited to temples and monasteries. Buddhism places special emphasis on real-life practice. Cultivation is the practice of the Dharma in daily life. Thus, a day's practice for a Buddhist looks something like this: from rising in the morning to going to bed in the evening, one interacts with others with speech, silence, action, and non-action. By following the example of the Buddha and the bodhisattvas, one takes compassion as one's own and expedient means to leading a rational life and dealing with others based on the Dharma.

Additionally, one can use his/her own time to focus on studies and to persevere. If space permits, one can place a Buddhist altar in one's home. Each morning after rising, one can offer flowers and water, light a stick of incense and pray, recite from the scriptures, or sit in meditation for five minutes before a Buddha or a bodhisattva image. At night before going to bed, a person can calm his/her mind before the image of the Buddha or recite Buddhist prayers while contemplating personal achievements and errors. Once or twice each week, one can attend religious practice at a temple, partaking of the joys of religion, and cleansing oneself of anger, greed, and afflictions while developing spiritual riches. Each day before a meal, one should join his/her palms and recite the four offerings, the Buddha's Light members' motto, or the five contemplations at mealtime to cultivate a spiritual sense of thankfulness and compassion.

In summary, practice does not mean practice in isolation for one's own sake. Practice should include going to temples, acquiring good knowledge, and seeking the Dharma. At the same time, one must strive to protect as well as spread the Dharma. This is the practice advocated by Humanistic Buddhism.

On
Education & Entertainment
the Way of Correct Living

Life is neither all work nor all cultivation. Life is like a plant that needs a number of things to grow, including air, water, and sun. In daily life, people cannot just work or rest without flexibility. In addition to three meals a day, the spiritual side of life must be attended to with education and amusement. Buddhist practitioners also need educational entertainment.

For example, when those who practice Chan are sitting in meditation, they must occasionally get up and walk around for the sake of body and mind. One who chants the name of the Buddha will also want to circumambulate and worship the Buddha. These are all sources of joy. One day each week Buddhist monastics take a day off. At dinner they need not wear their robes nor sing the *Offering Dharani* as they do for breakfast and lunch.

Among Buddhists, there are invariably some who like to travel, sightsee, and make pilgrimages, whereas others prefer nature, contemplating, meditating, and reflecting in solitude. There are even the sixteen contemplations in the *Sutra on Contemplation of the Buddha of Infinite Life*, which include observing sunrise, sunset, mountains, rivers, trees, scenery, Buddhas, and Buddhas' light, which are all considered amusements for the practitioner.

Those in the Pure Land "with baskets full of many wonderful flowers make offerings to the hundreds of thousands of millions of Buddhas in the other directions" in the morning, and idle and linger about at ordinary times amid seven rows of trees, seven tiers of railings, the waters of eight meritorious virtues, and proclaim the Buddha, the Dharma, and the Sangha with the birds, all of which is a joy for body and mind.

In the past, monastics were allowed to play chess as well as a game called "Picture of becoming a Buddha." In the game, the six Chinese characters used to write the words "Namo Amitabha Buddha" each had values for moving forward and backward, and moving in and out of the ten dharma realms. Those who played the game not only increased their knowledge of Buddhism but also had a good time and enhanced their friendships with those practicing the Way.

In addition to chess, monastics also practice the tea ceremony and calligraphy, as well as debate the sutras and practice the arts of transcribing the sutras, carving, painting, Buddhist dancing, and chanting. These are all educational ways to add a bit of spice to life.

There are twenty-four hours in a day. In addition to sleeping, eating, and working, appropriate forms of amusement for a change in pace are also important in life. For most people, amusement involves enjoying sights and sounds, gambling, and dynamic activities. Buddhism stresses nature; for example, Chan Master Niaoke lived in a tree, Chan Master Yuantong Na[77] lived in a mountain cave, while Chan Master Damei wore clothing made of water lily leaves and ate pine nuts. Emphasizing such a carefree life, how free and at ease they were! Chan masters have taught people to plant pine trees, pull weeds, till the land, and grow things, allowing our bodies and minds to merge with nature in the fields and our senses to roam in the sea of the mind, enjoying the tranquility of Dharma joys.

After Buddhism reached China, activities such as pilgrimages to mountains, worshipping sages, visiting noted monasteries and temples, and conversing with friends became very important. Through such activities, one could broaden good connections and increase experience. They, too, are part of Buddhist education and entertainment.

Today, education places equal emphasis on "morality and wisdom, the individual and the group, and education and amusement." From ancient times, Buddhism has placed equal emphasis on five types of education: practicing together in the temples for morality; listening to the sutras in the lecture halls for wisdom; doing chores for one's own physical health; following the six harmonious virtues of the sangha for group education; and carving, painting, and singing for aesthetic education.

Buddhism has many ways of "practicing religion while having fun," divisible into the following six general categories:

1) *Athletics*: walking meditation, making pilgrimages to various temples, traveling, Buddhist dancing, and practicing martial arts.

2) *Music*: singing, choir, playing musical instruments, traditional music, and storytelling.

3) *Arts*: calligraphy, sutra transcription, painting, carving, sculpture, and chess.

4) *Flowers and tea*: flower arrangement and tea ceremony.

5) *Labor*: working in nature, farming, working meditation, vegetable gardening, ascetic practice, and cooking.

6) *Practicing and upholding the Way*: looking for teachers, discussing the Way, reciting the Buddha's name, engaging in Chan joys and Dharma happiness, and meditating.

Besides clothing and food, and being warm and full with things from the material side of life, people also need to enhance life through art, service, and rest. How should lay devotees go about planning education and amusement? Any sort of amusement is appropriate as long as one does not give in to things that harm the spirit, such as wine, sex, money, and anger. For example, one can enjoy early morning exercise, music before bed, or taking time for walks and strolls during the day or when there is free time. Two or three good friends can get together to travel, chat, drink tea, talk about the Way, transcribe sutras, cook, or play music. Even dance and dinner parties among friends are permissible. However, all such activities should have their own conditions and purposes. For instance:

1) Those with whom one socializes with should all be good people.

2) The time for such activities should not exceed what is normal. For every twenty-four hours, work should occupy eight hours, sleep another eight hours, and the other eight hours are for eating, bathing, and amusement. There should be a balance.

3) Considerations of safety should determine the place for such activities. Disaster can occur in the mountains and at places with water; therefore, safety should be a prime consideration when going out. Gambling and over-consumption of alcohol are not appropriate forms of entertainment and should be avoided.

4) Husband and wife should attend all such activities together. Not only can they meet common friends and develop common interests, but they can also avoid the opportunity for extramarital affairs.

Since the Ming and Qing Dynasties, Buddhism has placed an emphasis on peaceful cultivation in temples and monasteries. This usually strikes people as cold, lonely, and without any feeling of human warmth. Most people think that Buddhism teaches emptiness, suffering, and impermanence of all things. For this reason, they think that the true study of Buddhism involves suffering and cutting oneself off from others. Actually, Buddhism is part of life and very active; it is a religion of vigor. Buddhism stresses daily life—in fact, everything from walking, dwelling, sitting, and sleeping to dressing, eating, and carrying firewood and water are all forms of the Dharma. The position taken by Humanistic Buddhism on education and amusement is that one should delve deeply into the scriptures in search of knowledge, but that one also must not forget that daily activities, such as eating, dressing, and sleeping, are also imbued with the Dharma. All one need do is apply oneself a little more in daily life to understanding, practicing, and experiencing this. Then "our lives will be imbued with Dharma happiness and not dissatisfaction with the ordinary happiness of the world."

On
Funerals & Celebrations
the Way of Right Views

If life is not happy, then it is sad. Traditionally, birth is viewed as a happy event and death as a cause for sadness. The birth of a son or daughter is something to celebrate; but death provokes cries of anguish and tears of sadness. Actually, at birth, a person is inevitably doomed to die. Since every person is born to die, wherein lies the happiness or sadness? When a person dies, it is like the coming of winter, but spring will come again, so where is the sadness? Birth and death are one. Birth entails death, and death leads to rebirth. The cycle of birth and death is endless and, for this reason, birth is not necessarily a happy event nor should death necessarily be the cause of sadness.

Since everyone is born and must die, ceremonies associated with these events are an important aspect of our lives. From ancient times, the Chinese have viewed birth and death as two important events in life. The filial devotion expressed by being thorough in planning funeral rites for parents and worshipping ancestors is a virtue inherent in Chinese culture and is in accord with the Buddhist notion of expressing gratitude.

However, in China, opinion on funeral rites varies greatly. There is no general agreement on these things, so many ideas and ways of doing things can and should be purified and improved. For instance, emphasis on practices such as using feng shui to select the burial day, waiting eight hours before placing the deceased in a coffin, and playing excessive music and having too many floats for funeral processions are not only a waste but also lessen the solemnity of the occasion. Therefore, in talking about funeral rites, right views must be established.

Although everyone must experience birth, old age, sickness, and death, few people face death calmly. On account of this, the important moment that occurs while on the verge of death is often neglected. It is a key moment for ascending to the upper realm or sinking to the lower realm; it is the most precious and decisive moment for determining one's future life. If the dying person's family members cry and carry on at that moment, causing sadness and making him/her lose the chance for a good rebirth, it is undoubtedly very harmful. As such, when someone passes away, it is inappropriate to cry excessively, to shake the person's body or stuff money into his/her hands, to make offerings of food at his/her feet, or to immediately change his/her clothes, because the consciousness of the deceased has not entirely departed. The person's consciousness may become reluctant to depart due to these actions, which may increase its suffering. When someone is critically ill, it is best to invite a Buddhist monastic or fellow practitioners to recite the sutras and the Buddhas' names along with family members to help guide the deceased to the Pure Land of Ultimate Bliss.[78] Elders who can speak the Dharma and who are respected by the dying can also be invited to comfort and enjoin the dying to single-mindedly contemplate the Buddha and seek rebirth in the Pure Land.

Modern burials require huge funeral plots and the erection of large tombs. This results in a conflict over land between the living and the dead. Buddhism, since its inception in India, has advocated cremation. Cremation is superior to burial, be it in the ground, sky, sea, or in trees. After the Buddha entered parinirvana, his body was cremated in the fire of samadhi. The idea of cremation has gradually become more widely accepted. After cremation, Buddhists will have their ashes housed in a pagoda, the best home to return to.

A Buddhist pagoda differs from an ordinary ossuary in that it not only solves space problems but also possesses profound significance for the faith. Therefore, the good works of Fo Guang Shan include the establishment of kindergartens, nursing homes, hospitals, and columbaria in which human remains can be kept. In this way, the birth, old age, sickness, and death of devotees can all be attended to according to Buddhist tradition.

With regard to funeral rites, it is important to pay attention to and refrain from the following:

1) *Vanity should have no part.* Nowadays, vanity plays an important role in handling funerals in that people want theirs to be better than others. This is unnecessary. What is most important is respecting the wishes of the deceased.

2) *Funerals should not be extravagant.* In a funeral, it should not matter how many musicians or floats you have or anyone else has. Funerals are a private household matter, so why involve so many others? Solemnity, grief, and respect are infinitely superior to a noisy funeral parade.

3) *Superstition should not play a role.* A funeral is nothing more than seeking peace for the departed and an expression of filialness by the living. Sincerity is all that is necessary.

Birth and death are two important events in life. Buddhism holds that birth is not entirely happy and death is not entirely sad. Both must be faced with a solemn attitude. Therefore, on the death of a relative or friend, mourning should be done solemnly; by the same token, a happy event should be celebrated simply.

According to the "Daxingren" part of the "Qiu Guan" section of the *Zhou Rites [Zhou Li]*,[79] "Celebrate the happiness of royalty with praise." These days any auspicious event is cause for happiness and deserves to be celebrated. Events such as marriage, the birth of a child, birthdays of seniors, a new house, a new book, passing the civil service exam, and a promotion are all worth celebrating. Whatever the event, it should be celebrated with simplicity and solemnity. If those participating can pay attention to the following rules of etiquette, then all will be happy:

1) For the celebration of any happy event, one should inform one's relatives and friends of the date, time, and place but

also avoid excess and the taking of life (e.g., by serving meat or fish at the reception).

2) When friends or relatives have a celebration, one should offer one's congratulations in person, by mail, or by telephone.

3) One should be on time for a celebration and avoid arriving late or leaving early.

4) One must dress, speak, and act properly for the occasion.

5) In selecting a gift, pay attention to its significance and usefulness. Buddhist books and prayer beads are good gifts.

Birth and death are two critical issues in life. There is an expression in the Chan School that says, "Not having been liberated from the cycle of birth and death is as grievous as when one mourns his or her parents." Birth and death are not just major events; they are also riddles to most people. The Buddha renounced his home and attained enlightenment for the truth behind these riddles. This is the focus of Buddhist teachings. Today's Humanistic Buddhism also aims to resolve the issues of birth and death. Birth involves nurturing and teaching; death involves conducting a funeral modestly.

In China, every place has its own unchanging habits and customs when it comes to dealing with important events such as death and marriage. Actually, many of the customs are superficial. Geomancy, feng shui, and emphasis on auspicious days are all based on superstitions. It is pointless to adhere too closely to them. Take auspicious days for example; if a day is bad, it is considered inauspicious. But how can any day really be bad? If it is daytime in Taiwan, it is nighttime in the United States. In regard to geomancy, some want a burial place facing east, west, or south, but in fact, there is no direction in space. For instance, when two people sit facing one another, one's right will be another's left, and one's view in the front will be another's view from the back. Which is which? On this account, the *Sutra on Upasaka Precepts* teaches that the Buddha informed Singalaka that there was no reason to worship the directions because there are no directions in space; instead, we should pay homage to the six directions in our minds.

The void contains no fixed compass points. Our true life extends throughout limitless space and time. When you attain awareness of your true nature, your mind will fill space, the dharma realms, the ten directions, the past, present, and future, and throughout the single entity of time and space. For this reason, there are no compass points in space, only in our minds.

The attitude that most people have in the face of something they do not understand, do not know, or cannot see is often one of pure speculation, exaggeration, and even superstition. People with such attitudes are subject to control by religious authority. Buddhism holds that all people possess Buddha Nature. This means that each and every one of us has sovereign rights and that from the beginning we are in charge of all that is ours. Although geomancy and feng shui have their own principles, these principles are not the truth. This is why Buddhism not only opposes geomancy but also superstition, and it advocates freeing oneself from religious authority. One should not harbor superstitions about time, nor cling to geomancy. Buddhism holds that "all days are good, and all places are good." With a good heart, any time and place will be good. Sincerity is far more important than superficiality.

On Nature

the Way of Environmental Protection

The word "natural" describes what happens in the world. Think of the cycle of the changing seasons; the cycle of birth, old age, sickness, and death experienced by all sentient beings; the shifting of thoughts from arising to abiding, changing and extinguishing; and the changes of matter from formation to abiding, destruction, and a return to emptiness. All of these are natural.

Nature has its laws, but they are not belabored or artificial; everything follows its naturally prescribed way. What the Buddha actually discovered when he attained enlightenment under the bodhi tree were the universal truths that "everything arises from dependent origination and the nature of all things is emptiness," which are the "natural" laws of the universe. From the principle of dependent origination were derived such concepts as, "the freedom of the power of karma," "the equality of all sentient beings," "the universal compassion of coexistence," and "the differentiation of birth and death." By unifying birth and death, a respect for life was brought fully into play.

Nature is like a circle. Good causes produce good effects; bad causes produce bad effects. Cause and effect follow one upon the other without beginning or end. Cause and effect and karmic retribution are truths of Buddhism. The Buddha was awakened to the truths of the universe, and his teachings explain the truth behind the workings of nature. This is why the Buddha often said "it is naturally so," meaning that things come from nature and are unforced.

Buddhism has always pursued the natural, stressing the human mind and human nature. For instance, the Buddha liked to stroll in secluded groves or to contemplate amid the tranquility of nature. Once, when Ananda was practicing meditation in the forest, he saw a hungry ghost and his mind was filled with compassion. While meditating under a tree, Subhuti experienced the profound significance of emptiness. Even the Chinese Chan masters embraced a natural life: they lived near rivers in the mountains far from the hustle and bustle and ties of life and were especially carefree in thought, bound by nothing–natural in a spiritual sense.

Natural implies harmony, while unnatural implies chaos. Ancient morality says, "Going against the current and struggling are illnesses of the mind." When greed, anger, ignorance, arrogance, and jealousy stir the mind, people will suffer. Buddhism teaches that everything arises and is extinguished due to conditions and follows nature. Buddhists view these states, such as having and not having, poverty and wealth, good and bad, and gain and loss, as all very natural. When everything follows nature, then it is like the Buddha: "When causes and conditions are ripe, Buddhas appear in the world; when causes and conditions cease, Buddhas enter parinirvana, coming and going for all sentient beings." This is natural. To follow nature and not be detained by afflictions and suffering is the environmental protection of body and mind.

Buddhism is a religion with a profound environmental consciousness. Not only does Buddhism stress protection of the spiritual environment of the mind but also the ecological balance in the world around us, being attentive, for example, to the protection of mountains and forests, rivers, ecosystems, and animals. The best example of environmental protection is found in the Western Pure Land of Ultimate Bliss. Amitabha Buddha is an environmental protectionist, and his Pure Land of Ultimate Bliss is solemnly and purely adorned with gold and has pavilions of seven jewels and seven tiers of railings. In addition to not having air or water pollution, noise pollution, poisonous gases, violence, or nuclear energy, when people think about food or clothing, their thoughts are gratified.

The most important goal is nothing less than the hope that all people can live and work naturally in peace and contentment. For it is only by following nature that our minds can achieve liberation and we can be free. Nature is the harmony among heaven, earth, and human beings. The suffering of most people arises as a result of conflicts that cannot be harmonized among human beings, events, objects, and places. When worldly affairs conform to nature, then there is life, growth, formation, beauty, and perfection. All life is closely linked to nature; it is part of nature. A natural life is not determined by being good or bad; it operates according to the principle of the cycle of birth and death. A natural way of living led the monk Dazhu Huihai[80] to say, "Eat when hungry, sleep when tired." The monk Yaoshan Weiyan[81] said, "Clouds are in the blue sky and water in a bottle." Clearly, the Way coexists with nature; the Way is to live naturally. Thus, all the great Buddhas rebuke those who do not smile when they should, those who are not happy when they should be, those who are not compassionate when they should be, those who do not speak when they should, and those who do not pay attention when good is spoken. The Buddha called them the five types of non-humans because their behavior does not conform to nature.

Nature is a kind of harmony; it is also a struggle. Through struggle, the rivers and oceans are untrammeled; lakes attain clarity only through purification; mountains must be stable; and trees must have roots to grow. Only by following nature can everything continue to exist.

Among all the things in this world, some are colorful and patterned, and some are plain. Some animals use camouflage as a means of self-defense, a natural response. Some animals are diurnal, others nocturnal. Some fly in the air on wings, while some move on land and others swim in the sea, all for the sake of existing in nature. Vicious death is also natural for some animals–this is what is referred to as natural selection. Although Buddhism urges us not to take life, it is still a matter of individual need. The truth is that it is not required of all organisms. This is a varied world; it is natural that some people are liberated and some dwell in the cycle of birth and death.

In the world of nature, flowers blossom beautifully, wither, and return to the soil for the benefit of other flowers. This is a natural cycle.

Therefore, birth, old age, sickness, and death, the arising, abiding, changing, and extinguishing, and formation, abiding, destruction, and extinction are all natural to this world. Going against heaven is unnatural. If people know how to live with nature, there is nothing to fear. If the soil is tilled and seeds are planted in the spring and summer, and if the grain is harvested and stored in the fall, there is nothing to fear in the winter. If lamps are prepared during the day, there is nothing to fear at nightfall.

In our daily lives, we encounter many natural and unnatural things. The natural brings joy to body and mind and everything proceeds smoothly; the unnatural leads to fatigue of body and mind, tiring oneself and harming others. In matters of emotion, balance and harmony are natural; in speaking, consideration and forgiveness are natural; in meeting with others, adhering to feelings or reason is natural; in using money, living within one's means is natural. Doing otherwise is unnatural.

When there is harmony among heaven, earth, and human beings, there is no distance between oneself and nature. Nature is the human mind, truth, and fate: the three bonds of the universe. In examining the histories of China or the West, we find that of all the kings and emperors in history, those who obeyed the will of heaven and the people succeeded, and those who did not were lost. Their rise and fall were closely linked to the principles of nature. Our own lives must also accord with nature if we are to be happy and harmonious. Thus, we cannot help but ask ourselves, "Can I conform to nature when I use money and live within my means? In emotional relationships, can I conform to nature and be balanced and harmonious? In speech, can I conform to nature and consider the needs of others? In doing things, does my attitude conform to nature and not go against the principles of reason?"

Nature should be followed; going against it will result in disaster. It is like never rising from bed, standing for a long time without sitting, working too long without rest, or being still for a long time without moving. All of these can result in physiological imbalances of the four great elements; people will grow ill, the root of health will be cut off, and eventually, they have to withdraw from the world. Over the last few centuries, because of excessive material consumption, humanity has gone too far and disturbed the environment, leading to the current ecological problems. This all goes to show that even the slightest violation of nature will result in bad effects.

It is much the same when it comes to dealing with people and social matters. If emotions follow one's own wishful thinking and run counter to nature, then they will not last; if wealth is gained through deceit or struggle, which runs counter to nature, then a fall is not far off; if fame is attained by misleading the public, which runs counter to nature, then one will be abandoned by others in the end; and if position is obtained without toil, which runs counter to nature, then there will be negative consequences.

If we wish to lead a wonderful life, then the laws of nature must be obeyed. Spouses should be respectful of and understand one another; among neighbors, friends, and relatives there should be amity; and colleagues should aid and support one another. To start a business, one should first conduct market surveys, raise capital, and make appropriate arrangements for human resources and management. To govern a nation, one should understand public opinion, employ loyal and honest people, carefully consider one's words, and diligently carry out good laws. Buddhists should set an example in fostering happiness and good ties, meditating and increasing wisdom, as well as shouldering the responsibility to instruct and guide all sentient beings. If one conforms to the Way in daily life–that is the Buddhist way of a natural life and way of living– then one will behave appropriately.

On Political Affairs

the Way of Political Participation

Government is the management of everyone's affairs. Humans are social animals and cannot exist alone; thus, our collective affairs must be taken into account, making government important.

Most people associate government with power, strategy, political parties, and struggle. Therefore, Buddhists who stress harmony and pacifism tend to avoid discussions of political affairs. Some people advocate the separation of religion and state, further distancing religion from politics.

In actuality, political participation is the right of every citizen, except for felons who have been deprived of this right. Even Buddhist monastics must pay taxes and do military service to fulfill their obligations as citizens. Renunciation does not imply leaving the country, and Buddhism advocates not only personal liberation but the liberation of others as well. While different, Buddhism and government both have something of value to offer, and one can complement and complete the other. Government needs to be supplemented with the educating influence of Buddhism, while Buddhism can be spread with the protection and support of government.

Historically, Buddhism has never separated itself from and has always maintained good relations with the government. After the

Buddha became enlightened, he spread the Dharma to other countries and often spoke in royal courts, leading to just government. The rulers of many Indian states such as Bimbasara, Ajatasatru, Prasenajit, and Udayana were converted to and took refuge in Buddhism. Later they all became the Dharma-protectors of Buddhism and used Buddhist truths to govern the state, perfect society, and aid the people. After the Buddha entered parinirvana, many kings, such as Asoka, Kaniska, Siladitya, and Milinda, followed the teachings of the Buddha, ruled in accordance with the Dharma, and established just governments, adding glorious pages to the history of India.

Throughout the history of China, monastics and emperors had close cooperative interaction. A number of those who assisted the court were elevated to the status of imperial masters, such as Nanyang Huizhong,[82] Fazang Xianshou,[83] Qingliang Cheng'guan,[84] Wuda Zhixuan,[85] Yulin Tongxiu,[86] and Tiantai Zhiyi.[87] Others held ministerial positions, such as Huilin, who was invited to serve as prime minister by Emperor Wen of the Song Dynasty. Every day, he handled many important affairs of state and was widely known as the "Prime Minister in Black Robes." Emperor Taizong of the Tang Dynasty[88] sought advice from Master Mingzhan on how to provide the nation with peace and stability. Mingzhan advised him to take compassion as his principal aim. Emperor Taizong was delighted and made him a minister. During the Ming Dynasty, Yao Guangxiao[89] was known as Chan Master Daoyan. Emperor Yongle,[90] appreciating his outstanding abilities, issued a decree ordering him to return to secular life to assist the imperial court. His contributions to the peaceful and happy fate of the nation were enormous at the beginning of the Ming Dynasty.

In the Wei-Jin and the Northern and Southern Dynasties, the court established a number of official religious positions that are still in use in Japan today. Until recently, Tibet was governed by a theocracy. In Thailand, Sri Lanka, and Nepal, "Buddhism leads the government, and the government respects Buddhism." In Japan, Buddhism is the state religion, and all Japanese citizens and members of the government must respect the Triple Gem. The Korean government also made Buddhism the state religion and had the entire Buddhist Canon carved for the sake of the nation. All these examples serve to show the intimate relationship between Buddhism and government. Governments need the assistance and culture of Buddhism. As Dr. Sun Yat-sen once commented, "The benevolence of Buddhism is in emancipating the world; the Dharma can compensate for deficiencies in the law."

Buddhism not only has the ability to harmonize government, but can also be an aid to government when it comes to transforming and guiding the remotest parts of the nation, eliminating hatred, converting the recalcitrant through persuasion, and teaching through compassion. For example, the five precepts can be very useful in providing the nation with peace and stability as the *Ritual of the Triple Gem Refuge and Five Precepts Ceremony* [*Sangui Wujie Zheng Fan*] notes, "If ten people in a village of a hundred families uphold the precepts, then ten people will be pure; if one hundred people in a state of a thousand households cultivate the 'ten wholesome conducts,' then one hundred people will be on friendly terms; if this teaching is spread to a thousand households, then the benevolent will number in the thousands. By practicing one virtue, one evil is eliminated, and so is one punishment; if one punishment is eliminated, then ten thousand punishments within a state can be eliminated. This is creating peace without striving for it."

There are many historical records of the influence and contributions of Buddhism to government. Some examples include assisting in production, developing transportation, protecting the environment, cultural planning and development, building housing for troops, founding schools, raising money for hospitals, managing financial affairs, and contributing to science and literature.

In the midst of war, Buddhism has played a role in resisting aggression and working for stability. For example, the Buddha proclaimed to Varsakara,[91] minister of the state of Magadha, the establishment of a national "seven forms of not retreating," skillfully transforming a bloody war. In the days of the An Lushan rebellion during the Tang Dynasty, frequently there were insufficient military supplies. As a result, Buddhists sold monastic certificates to raise funds for the military, contributing greatly to the pacification of the rebellion. When Emperor Gaozong of the Southern Song[92] moved south of the Yangsi River, he invited Chan Master Fadao to join the imperial court and assist with national affairs.

He was able to stabilize the military situation through his strenuous efforts to obtain grain for the army, and also by taking part in military expeditions and making strategic contributions. When the Mongolian people entered the Central Plains, Yelu Chucai, an advisor to the Mongol Khan, employed the sagely talents of a Chan monk by the name of Liu Bingzhong and drafted him as a minister. In order to protect the lives and property of the Han Chinese[94] and avoid execution, Liu Bingzhong[93] helped set up the imperial court system and assisted Yelu Chucai with the establishment of Han culture, ensuring the livelihood of the Han people. Chan Master Zhiwen of the Yuan Dynasty so moved the Kublai Khan through his civilized grace that the title Chan Master Foguo Puan was bestowed upon him. Clearly, there are countless historical examples from ancient times to the present of how Buddhism assisted and educated governments.

The Buddha's teachings on benevolent leadership are scattered throughout the scriptures. For example, in the *Sutra on the Prophecy of Mahasatya's Enlightenment* [*Bodhisattva Gocaropaya Visaya Vikurvananirdesa Sutra*], the Buddha instructed that rulers should be as concerned about the people as a mother about her children and that they should never be out of their minds. In the *Sutra of Buddha's Discourse to King Prasenajit* [*Rulai Shijiao Shengjun Wang Jing*], the Buddha tells the King, "In dealing with the people of the world, the ruler should adopt the four means of embracing so that servants might carry out their duties and ministers can assist." According to the *Long Discourses of the Buddha*, "Rulers and ministers should work together and respect one another. If this can be done, then the nation will enjoy perpetual peace." It is recorded in the *Commentary on the Bei Sutra* [*Fo Shuo Bei Jing Chao*], "To be an enlightened ruler, one must understand the past and know the present, know when to act and when not to, when to be firm and when to yield, humble oneself and benefit the people, and give alms equally." The *Treasury of Truth with Parables* also points out five things a ruler must do: 1) lead the people without oppressing them, 2) support, educate, and strengthen scholar-officials, 3) consider and practice good virtues, 4) trust ministers who are honest and direct, and 5) not to be fond of playing or fooling around. The *Sutra of Golden Light* [*Suvarnaprabhasttama Sutra*] states, "All should be treated equally, family or not. To be a king of the true Dharma, no one party within the nation should be favored. The title 'Dharma king' resounds throughout the three realms."

The teachings of Buddhism and the activities of monastics can influence a ruler's idea of government and establish a propitious and harmonious society. The authority of kings can help spread Buddhism, purifying the morals of the time and the people's minds. Venerable Master Daoan[95] of the Jin Dynasty said, "Without the support of the king, the Dharma would be difficult to propagate." In the *Sutra on the Prajna-Paramita for the Benevolent King*, the Buddha entrusts the protection of the Dharma to the king by virtue of the fact "those below will emulate those above as the grass bends to the wind." During the Buddha's lifetime, due to kings such as Bimbasara and Prasenajit, Buddhism spread across India. After the Buddha entered parinirvana, King Asoka erected eighty-four thousand stupas and dispatched teachers to Ceylon (Sri Lanka) and other places to spread the Dharma far and wide. Emperor Ming of the Eastern Han Dynasty dispatched Cai Yin, an official, to India in order to invite eminent monks such as Kasyapa-matanga and Dharmaraksa to China to propagate the Dharma. The translation of Buddhist scriptures into Chinese was done with the patronage of the imperial court and the establishment of translation centers. For example, Kumarajiva received the support of Emperor Yao Xing[96] of the latter Qin Dynasty who put the Ximing Pavilion[97] at his disposal for translating the sutras. He translated the *Lotus Sutra* and the *Treatise on the Middle Way* [*Madhyamika Sastra*] along with 384 other fascicles. With the support of Emperor Taizong of the Tang Dynasty, Master Xuanzang translated the *Sutra of Great Wisdom* [*Mahaprajnaparamita Sutra*] and the *Treatise on the Demonstration of Mind-Only* [*Vidyamatrasiddhi Sastra*] along with 1,335 other fascicles, permitting the Dharma to shine resplendently throughout China.

With today's freedom of religion and the protection and support of the government, Buddhists can assert a purifying influence on government. For this reason, Buddhism needs the support of government, and government should not be jealous of Buddhism; nor should Buddhism attend to trifling matters while neglecting essentials and only rewarding philanthropy. Instead, it ought to encourage all activities that purify the mind and improve the social climate. Buddhism must also be directly concerned with society, defending human rights and the happiness and welfare of the people. As such, Buddhists should not seek to remain aloof from politics. The individual need not care about position, fame, and power, but cannot forsake concern for society or the responsibility of serving others. In order to spread the Dharma and benefit others, Buddhists today should not seek to avoid politics but should be actively involved and do their share. For in society, who can avoid politics? Although Buddhists may not wish to be involved, they must be concerned about society and politics. The appropriate attitude for a Buddhist today is "ask after government without interfering in governance."

On International Affairs

the Way of Tolerance

Owing to modern technological developments, global communications have become more convenient, which has succeeded in eliminating distance between people. Telephones, the Internet, and electronic mail are all bringing the people of the world closer together, making the 21st century the age of the "global village." All human beings can now boast about being "world citizens."

In the global village, progress cannot be hindered even though there are many nations, peoples, cultures, and languages. Throughout the nations, cities, and towns of the world there are many communities. In each community, there are a number of households, families, personalities, ages, genders, languages, customs, and religious beliefs coexisting side by side, none of which disrupt social harmony. This is true from the smallest community to the global village. All people love their family first, then their clan, neighbors, village, society, nation, their compatriots, humankind, and then all sentient beings. The closer a relationship is, the deeper the love; the more distant the relationship is, the weaker the affection. Thus, the idea of "unconditional loving-kindness and great compassion to all as one" advocated by Buddhism is actually difficult for most people to practice, hence the difference between the sage and the ordinary person.

For most people, love and compassion have causes and conditions, especially when it comes to relatives and the distinctions between love and hate and oneself and others. As a result of these comparisons, haggling, disputes, and fighting arise among people. The Humanistic Buddhist view of international relations seeks to eliminate drawing distinctions between oneself and others and instead bring about an awareness of "oneness and coexistence," of mutual tolerance, respect, equality, harmony, and of working together and sharing.

For example, Buddhism speaks of the three time periods: past, present, and future; in space, there is here, there, and the ten directions; in this world, there are countless beings born of the womb, eggs, moisture, and transformation. The Buddhist worldview has already entirely eliminated distinctions in time and space.

The *Amitabha Sutra* states, "Each living being of that land, with baskets full of many wonderful flowers, makes offerings to the hundreds of thousands of millions of Buddhas of other directions." This forming of ties and mutual praise is a fully international view. In the *Sutra on the Ascent of Maitreya [Mi'le Pusa Shangsheng Jing]* and the *Sutra on the Decent of Maitreya [Mi'le Pusa Xiasheng Jing]*, Maitreya not only interacts with the people of earth, but also in the three realms in the twenty-eight heavens and the eighteen hells where he liberates countless beings. Sadaparibhuta Bodhisattva treats all sentient beings without distinction; and Avalokitesvara Bodhisattva travels through all lands liberating beings. Buddhism is particularly concerned about weak and powerless groups and small, underdeveloped nations.

When eating, Buddhists make offerings to all sentient beings. For the smallest things, we thank all beings in the ten directions. Buddhism advocates equality; the Buddha treated all sentient beings as if they were Rahula, his beloved son. Buddhism stresses protecting the right to life for all sentient beings, which is why Buddhism has never been the cause of a war.

People say that since ancient times, those who have traveled the world over have been soldiers, merchants, explorers, and Buddhist monastics, seeking teachers and the Way. One history of the relations between China and India relates the story of the thousands of Buddhist monastics and lay followers who walked the Silk Road. Another history of the relations between China and Japan tells of the great numbers of people who crossed the sea between the two countries. One Mahayana scripture states, "To embrace three thousand worlds in one thought, the mind contains the great void." All the Buddhas and bodhisattvas come and go among the worlds of the ten directions.

In the thirty years since tourism was first widely encouraged in Taiwan, Buddhists have organized tour groups to all parts of the world. With contact across the Taiwan Strait, Taiwanese Buddhists have flocked to Mainland China to make pilgrimages to famous mountain temples. I have led a number of groups to India, Nepal, and the United States and once set a ten-stage itinerary for seeing different parts of the world. It includes:

1. Taiwan
2. Singapore, Malaysia, and Thailand
3. Japan and Korea
4. South Africa
5. United States and Canada
6. Australia and New Zealand
7. Europe
8. Russia
9. India
10. Mainland China

In addition, Fo Guang Shan often organizes international academic conferences and trips, such as a trip to the Vatican to meet with the Pope and trips to mosques, all with the hopes of sowing peace throughout the world.

I once said that because Taiwan was able to develop its science and technology, it enjoys prosperity, but only in a material sense. Spiritual poverty, chaos, and sickness have also spread. Buddhists emphasize internal purity and thereby recognize that the roots of inequality in the world stem from ignorance and clinging to the notion of a self. The human desires for power and fame are also rooted there. Greed leads to mutual conflict, bringing about perpetual struggle. Buddhism teaches us that in order to root out chaos in the world, we must start by purifying the mind. World peace is possible only by realizing peace in our minds and by practicing the Buddhist teachings of non-self, compassion, respect, and peace.

The United Nations has repeatedly advocated peace. Peace has been the dream of every person since ancient times. Confucianism's Great Harmony for the world is the hope for world peace and happiness. Dr. Sun Yat-sen took the idea of "one world for all" as his ideal in establishing the Republic. Buddhism sees the ideal of "one family under heaven, and I am no different from others" as a way to establish a Pure Land on earth for the four forms of birth and the nine realms of existence, which are all equal in the dharma realms.

"People should care for the aged and the young as if they were family" is the traditional Chinese concept of love without distinction. In addition to protecting human rights, Buddhism goes one step further by considering that all sentient beings have the right to life. Buddhism respects the right to life because "all sentient beings possess Buddha Nature" and "all are future Buddhas." Buddhism's advocacy for the right to life of all sentient beings naturally transcends national boundaries to see the world as one beyond all divisions, one in which we are all the same.

The *Subcommentary on the Flower Ornament Sutra* [*Huayan Jing Sui Shu Yanyi Chao*] teaches, "The mind, the Buddha, and all sentient beings are all the same." Mutual respect, forgiveness, equality, non-self, and compassion among sentient beings are the ideals needed by all peoples and nations. Because we all reside on this earth, we should have the same hopes of living together and promoting the idea of equality between the Buddha and sentient beings, the sage and the ordinary, and oneself and others, and of eliminating the divisions between peoples and nations. Everyone should adopt the international perspective of "extending in the ten directions and throughout the three time periods," taking "the world as a single family" as their starting point. This will allow everyone to embrace the dharma realms and become citizens of the world, protecting the environment and caring for all resources. By treating others as we would like to be treated, we can enlighten ourselves as well as others, improve life and have faith, form good affinities with all sentient beings, be socially compassionate, and bring light to the world. Only in this way can we promote world peace together.

On the Future

the Way of Development

The saddest thing in life is when a person has no hope for the future. Without hope, there is no future. People live on hope. People have children to make provisions for old age; they raise and educate them hoping that they will be successful. Strengthening family ties and living in harmony with neighbors implies hope that we can all live together better in the future; planting trees and flowers and storing grain in the event of famine also exhibit a sense of boundless hope. The Chinese are concerned about continuing the family line over generations in hopes of extending the life of the people. Even today's organ transplants are a hope to extend life.

People willingly pay taxes with the hope that the nation will improve in the future. Bridges and roads are repaired in the hope that transportation will become more convenient. Welfare is provided with the hope to relieve poverty, that the social welfare system will not be lacking. The capable and wise are elected with the hope that government will become increasingly more democratic. Punishing corrupt officials is done with the hope that government will become impartial. Everybody today hopes that there will be good weather for crops, the country will be prosperous, people will live in peace, and that the world will soon know peace.

Buddhism not only speaks of the past but also of the future. It places a good deal of emphasis on the future because the future is our hope. In many Buddhist scriptures, the Buddha foretells how much time will elapse and in what world his disciples will become Buddhas and what their names will be. This is a clear indication of how seriously Buddhism views the future. Buddhism often speaks of "vows." Many Buddhists vow to be reborn in a certain world where they will serve all sentient beings. A vow is indicative of how Buddhists value the future. Those who repeat the Buddha's name hope to one day be reborn in the Pure Land; Chan Buddhists hope to attain enlightenment; those who give alms, form good affinities, and transfer merits all do so with the hope that things will be better in the future.

People live on hope. The lives of people who live with hope have meaning. Those who give up do so because they have lost hope. Only with hope is there a future. Life without a future is like a beautiful dusk, the beauty of which will be diminished by its short span.

A child learns how to behave from his or her parents. In school, a child acquires knowledge in hope of a good future. People work during the day and put in overtime in the evening in hope of a better tomorrow. Animals hibernate in winter because they have hope for a better future; ants and bees also store food for the future. Seeing children and young adults, one has hope for the future of the nation. Although plants go dormant in the winter, their roots are still alive so that life might spring anew in the future.

The future sees the continuity of life, an unending river forever flowing. A person who lives a day will make plans for the next hundred years. Though the span of life is brief, it returns to the boundless future.

People save and work for the future. The future is a beautiful hope. Science has made progress for the future, to improve the future of all human beings. Philosophers propose philosophical ideals to enrich human thought; writers create, praising the perfect future. Industrialists produce to improve the lot of humanity. Many revolutionaries sacrificed themselves for their hopes for the future. Humanity struggles for the future, filling it with boundless promise and beauty.

People willingly work and suffer in the present for the sake of the future. People work diligently today for the sake of a happy future.

People hope for the future success of their children and happiness of their family. People work hard so that they can retire later with a pension. People plant and sow today for a harvest in the future. For a good reputation in the future, people establish themselves today. People diligently render meritorious service, achieve virtue, and express themselves in writing to gain a place for themselves in history.

We all live with the hope for a better tomorrow. There are many things to do tomorrow, so we rest well today. For success in the future, we diligently sow good things in this life. We must live in hope and not in memory, because the future is more beautiful than the present. Only with the future is there unbounded hope.

If we look at the Buddhist concepts of the three time periods and cause and effect, we see that there is more to life than just the present. The present exists because of the past, and the future exists because of the present. And with the future, there are the three time periods; with the three time periods comes hope. The three time periods are the past, present, and future. People not only study the historical past, they study the sciences and social sciences of the present, always with an eye to the future, and that is why there are futuristic studies.

Futurism is a study of the unknown. Contemporary society is in a state of perpetual flux, the future as yet unfixed. How can it be studied? Futurism involves making predictions about the future based on thinking about and studying the human past and present.

The future of humanity, war, economics, biology, and space are universal topics of study. It is safe to say that all scholars are looking to the future. Humans are already planning to occupy outer space; biologists are studying ways of extending human life. Geographers are leading people to open up wastelands and deserts; others are looking at ways of changing floodwater into oil and how to repair bad genes.

In the future, there will be missions to the moon, Mars, and Jupiter. People will be able to eat the air, and tree leaves will be used to cure hunger. Stones and bricks will be made into bread and wood into shredded meat. People will only need one meal a day and will be able to use a remote control from their beds to influence the world.

None of this is impossible. The Internet, faxes, electronic mail, and information technology have changed human life, shrinking the distance between people. The discovery of genes and the code of life only serves to underscore the advanced and accurate nature of the Buddhist theory of the power of karma.

The supernatural power[98] of the clairvoyant, or the Deva-eye, which allows everything to be seen, regardless of obstacles or distance, is often mentioned in Buddhism. The power of the clairaudience, or the Deva-ear, allows everything to be heard, regardless of distance in both time and space. This sounds more like the stuff of myth. Today, with the use of television satellites, we can see the world regardless of where we may be. Isn't this clairvoyance? With the aid of broadcast stations and telephones, we can hear regardless of distance. Isn't this clairaudience? People sit on flying carpets in the *Arabian Nights*, and they can fly wherever they want to go. Crystal balls allow people to see the future. Isn't this the stuff of myth? But don't airplanes resemble flying carpets? Don't televisions resemble crystal balls? There was a time when all these things seemed like myths. These myths were foreseen in the Buddhist scriptures.

When we look at the *Amitabha Sutra*, we see that the Pure Land of Ultimate Bliss is paved with gold, the water runs hot and cold, and the birdsong and sound of flowing waters speak the Dharma. In the World of Ultimate Bliss, there are no traffic jams, there is no lust, and people can fly; thoughts and sights are filled with joy. Long ago, Buddhism depicted a beautiful future where everything is as one could wish it.

"A society pervaded by the Buddha's light" is the ideal future society for Buddhism. What is meant by a society pervaded by the Buddha's light is a pure land in this world, with a government for the protection of all life and a religion of truth. The pure land spoken of by Buddhism is not just the Western Pure Land of the Amitabha Buddha, the Pure Land of the Medicine Buddha,[99] or the million other Buddha Lands. The pure land of Buddhism is something that can be made manifest in this world today. As the *Vimalakirti Sutra* states, "Where the mind is pure, the land is pure." This means that although the world is dirty, chaotic, dark, unstable, and filled with affliction, it is just an expression of our imperfect minds. If our minds achieve perfection, then the future will be pervaded by the Buddha's light and never again will our society have class conflicts; men, women, and all beings will be equal. There will be no haves or have-nots, and life will be free from worry. There will not be bad people to stir up trouble, nor will there be government oppression. Society will be stable and happy. Thus, the World of Ultimate Bliss can be realized before our very eyes, and our society can become a pure land.

A pure land in this world is the ideal society for the future. To achieve this ideal, everyone must uphold the five precepts. The five precepts are the basic commandments of Buddhism. They are: 1) do not kill, 2) do not steal, 3) do not engage in sexual misconduct, 4) do not lie, and 5) do not use drugs and intoxicants. Although five precepts are taught: do not violate the rights of sentient beings. Instability, chaos, and struggle arise because people violate the rights of others and do not respect one another. All we need to do is uphold the five precepts. We must respect and not violate all sentient beings' right to life. We must not steal or violate the property of others. No sexual misconduct means to respect and not violate the body and name of others. To not lie means to respect and not violate the reputation of others. Not using drugs and intoxicants means that we will respect and not violate our own bodies, health, and reasoning. If everyone can strictly adhere to the five precepts, practice the four means of embracing and the six perfections, and fully understand cause and effect, karmic retribution, and the Noble Eightfold Path, then it will not be difficult to realize the pure land.

The span of human life stretches from the past to the present and from the present into the future. The road of life from birth to death lasts just a few decades, but birth leads to death and death to rebirth, time and time again into the future.

What does the future hold? What will it be like? Most people hope not only for a beautiful future, but to know what is coming in advance. Therefore, many seek assistance from fortunetellers and diviners. What does the future hold? The future is without beginning or end! It is like a clock, ticking on and on, and no one knows when it will come to a halt. It is a riddle that cannot be solved. Despite knowing that the future is without beginning or end, why are we so calculating about the present? How much of the limitless future can this life of a hundred years or so account for? Therefore, true Buddhists do not concern themselves with fortunetellers or divination. There is no need to because the future cannot be known. If we really want to know the future, then simply take hold of it. The *Sutra on the Cause and Effect of the Three Time Periods* asserts, "If you want to know the causes of the past life, they are to be found in this life; if you want to know the effects of the next life, they are to be made in this life." Therefore, any cause will produce a similar effect. All people are free to decide their own life.

There is no better way to know the future than to take hold of life now. In life, there is past, present, and future. Actually, the past is not wholly past for it influences our present life. Although the present does not stop, it leads us into the future. The future continues to unfold, life after life, without end. In a broad sense, the past is innumerable kalpas long; broadly speaking, the future is also innumerable kalpas long. We can consider our past behavior and learn from it to improve the future. We cannot stop the present and be complacent, because without taking the next step, how can we arrive at the future? The value of life is not found solely in the past but even more so in the future, because the future is everyone's hope. When we sow what we hope to harvest and when we see the sun set in the west, we hope that it will rise as usual in the east. People live with hope for the future. Knowing that there is the possibility for happiness in the future makes the suffering of the present easier to bear. If there are no ideals, why talk about goals or achievements? Without a future, there can be no goals or ideals, nor the satisfaction of attaining them.

Therefore, the Buddhist conception of the three time periods and cause and effect supply us with boundless hope for the future. The three time periods include past lives, this life, and future lives, as well as the past, present, and future and even one moment ago, this very moment, and the next moment. The three time periods are encompassed in a single thought and in our minds. If we can grasp the past, present, and future with good thoughts and deeds, then we can ensure a bright future and a full and complete life.

Buddhism makes a distinction between mundane Dharma and supramundane Dharma. Although the ultimate aim of Buddhism is the pursuit of nirvana and spiritual liberation, people cannot escape from mundane

Dharma. The Dharma advocates "first entering the world in order to leave it." Hence, "Seek the Dharma and enlightenment in this world; seeking wisdom apart from this world is like looking for horns on a rabbit." People cannot exist apart from this world and must live in it. Most people live a:

1. Material life–because material things account for a great part of our lives.

2. Life of emotions–because humans are animals with senses; this is the reason for the Buddhist term "sentient beings."

3. Collective life–because humans are social animals.

4. Life of the bodily senses–because most people rely on their six senses (eyes, ears, nose, tongue, body, and mind) to pursue the happiness associated with the six sense objects (form, sound, smell, taste, touch, and dharma).

Although most people lead material, emotional, and collective lives of the bodily senses, they should remember that:

1. Material things are limited and our boundless desires can never be satisfied. For this reason, we must live sensible, economical lives.

2. There are shortcomings to emotions; they will not leave us satisfied forever. Therefore, we must attempt to purify our emotions.

3. Collective life also means inevitable conflict. Therefore, we should live according to the six points of reverent harmony.

4. The bodily senses are impermanent; they arise and are extinguished due to causes and conditions. Therefore, we should live a life of faith and joy in the Dharma.

The above is a Humanistic Buddhist blueprint for life and absolutely necessary for the realization of a Humanistic Buddhist Pure Land. The section entitled "The Buddha Way" of the *Vimalakirti Sutra* offers a summation of Humanistic Buddhism:

Wisdom is the mother of all bodhisattvas,

Skillful means the father;
All guides and teachers
Are born of such parents.

Joy in the Dharma is their spouse,
Compassion is their daughter,
Goodness and sincerity their sons;
Home is the contemplation of the void.

The passions are disciples,
Controlled at will.
Dharma is their good friend
Through which enlightenment is attained.

The six perfections are their companions,
The four means of embracing their musicians;
Music and song are
The teachings of the Dharma.

Their garden is planted with
The trees of no outflows,
The flowers of enlightenment,
The fruit of the wisdom of liberation.

Their pool of eight liberations
Is filled with the water of concentration,
Planted with the lotuses of the seven purities;
It is where the pure bathe.

The five supernatural powers are their draft animals,
Their vehicle the Mahayana,
Their driver one mind,
Their road the Noble Eightfold Path.

Their appearances are solemn,
Their ornaments auspicious,
Their clothing good conscience,
Their garlands virtuous aspiration.

Their wealth is the seven kinds of Dharma treasures,
And their teachings enrich others;
All their speech and cultivation
Are dedicated to the great benefit.

Their bed is the four meditations,
Where the pure way of life is born;
Their enlightenment comes from
Constantly learning and increasing wisdom.

Their food is the sweet dew of the teachings,
Their drink the juice of liberation;
Their bath is the pure mind,
The precepts their perfume.

Having conquered all afflictions,
They are invincible.
Having subdued the four Maras,
They raise their standards on the field of enlightenment.

They are willingly born
Though they know of no arising or extinction.
They appear in all the Buddha realms
Like an omnipresent sun above.

Though they worship the countless Buddhas
In the ten directions,
They never dwell on the slightest difference
Between themselves and the Buddhas.

The proof for Humanistic Buddhist theory is in the Buddhist scriptures. The Buddha's teachings are filled with humanism, and Humanistic Buddhism is in fact the Buddha's original concern. Therefore, it can be said that two and a half millennia ago, the Buddha had already fully drawn up the Humanistic Buddhism blueprint for life for the sake of all sentient beings. The question up to now has been how to propagate Humanistic Buddhism and realize the blueprint. This is what all followers of the Buddha ought to be diligently working toward.

I do not think that Humanistic Buddhism can simply remain on a conceptual level; it must be actively realized. For this reason, over the last thirty years Fo Guang Shan has steadfastly maintained the four directives of "using culture to propagate the Dharma, education to develop talent, philanthropy to benefit society, and community practice to purify the mind" to realize the Dharma in different areas.

In the area of culture, in addition to the ongoing editing of the Buddhist Canon, the 1989 gold-medal winning *Fo Guang Buddhist Encyclopedia* was completed after many years of work. It is an immense resource for Buddhists at home and abroad. The *Chinese Buddhist Sutra Series* renders the scriptures into modern vernacular language, making them accessible and understandable to one and all. Five years ago, for the sake of sincere students of Buddhism, I organized a group of about one hundred people to compile the *Buddhist Reference Books* and the *Fo Guang Buddhist Textbooks* to be used as systematic introductions to Buddhism.

In 2000, Fo Guang Shan founded the *Merit Times*, as well as edited the *Universal Gate Buddhist Journal, Chinese Buddhist Academic Series*, and a series of books on *Chinese Buddhist Cultural Essays* to encourage research on Buddhism. Beautiful Life Television now provides visual channels of communication for Buddhism and a way to transmit the Dharma to all on a daily basis. Cultural enterprises, such as *Gandha Samudra Culture Company, Fo Guang Cultural Enterprise*, and *Oracle Records Company*, all publish periodicals for laypersons and scholars alike. Modern media are being utilized to propagate the Dharma and benefit sentient beings.

In the area of education, in addition to founding sixteen Buddhist academies, four universities, twenty-six libraries, and nine art galleries to develop talent, we have held Buddhist examinations to further promote the study of Buddhism around the world. Various academies and temples also hold summer camps, Buddhist conferences, urban Buddhist academies, and Sunday schools for kids to sow the seeds of wisdom in all corners of the globe.

In the area of philanthropy, the Great Compassion Children's Home, the Charitable Medical Corps, and retirement homes and cemeteries have all been established for taking care of the newborn, the aged, the sick, and the deceased. In the area of teaching and practice, at the same time every Saturday throughout the world, Fo Guang Shan holds an Amitabha Chanting Service. And in response to local demands, the regularly scheduled practice sessions, the ten plus meditation halls, recitation halls, scriptoriums, and ceremonial halls are effectively working to purify people's minds.

In my own life, I have done my utmost to promote Humanistic Buddhism. When I lecture on the sutras, I want everyone to understand; when I write articles, I want them to be accessible to everyone; in establishing temples, I want people to be able to use them; in organizing activities, I want everyone to be able to attend; in organizing Dharma services, I want everyone to experience Dharma joy; and in propagating Buddhism overseas, I insist upon providing translation resources. I try to meet the needs of the people, whatever the time and place. This is because the Buddhism that people need is practical Buddhism.

Back in 1954, in order to meet the demands of the time and the needs of sentient beings, I proposed the printing of hardbound Buddhist books and teaching on the streets. Gradually, I spread Buddhism to jails and schools and spoke on radio and television. I also organized Taiwan's first Buddhist choir to help spread the teachings throughout the island. Over the last forty years, I have diligently turned the temples into lecture halls and textbooks into Buddhist reading materials; I have taken private practice and made it collective; I have made the recitation of sutras into lectures on sutras; and in order to get lay followers involved in the propagation of Buddhism, I established the Buddha's Light International Association and a lecturer system in the hope that the Humanistic Buddhist Blueprint for Life could gradually be realized under the radiating light of the Buddha.

Finally, after many years of hard work and the assistance of devotees everywhere, Fo Guang Shan has made many contributions that are worthy of pride. For example:

- The number of Buddhists in Taiwan has increased
- More young people are studying Buddhism

- Lay followers are propagating Buddhism
- Humanistic Buddhism is widely accepted
- The media takes Buddhism seriously
- Buddhist artifacts are widely viewed
- Buddhist hymns are respected
- The number of Buddha's Light Association members has increased dramatically
- Academia has affirmed Buddhism
- Politicians are practicing Buddhism
- Performers are taking refuge in Buddhism
- Buddhist exam results are excellent.

Fo Guang Shan has influenced and changed Buddhism in Taiwan:

- From traditional Buddhism to modern Buddhism
- From individual Buddhism to collective Buddhism
- From Buddhist hymns to Buddhist songs
- From a penitent Buddhism to an enterprising Buddhism
- From regional Buddhism to international Buddhism
- From disorganized Buddhism to systematic Buddhism
- From passive Buddhism to active Buddhism
- From secluded Buddhism to societal Buddhism
- From Buddhism that avoids the world to Buddhism that benefits and engages the world
- From monastic Buddhism to monastic and lay Buddhism
- From a Buddhism of followers to a Buddhism of lecturers
- From a Buddhism of temples to a Buddhism of meeting halls
- From a sectarian Buddhism to a widely accepted Buddhism
- From a Buddhism of good deeds to a missionary Buddhism of advocacy
- From a Buddhism of Dharma services to a Buddhism of activities
- From a Buddhism of elders to a Buddhism of youth

All these successes serve to demonstrate that regardless of how good the Dharma is, it must meet the needs of society and benefit the people if it is to have any value. Promoting Humanistic Buddhism really means getting people to practice Humanistic Buddhism; it has to be more than just slogans.

Humanistic Buddhism is the future mainstream of Buddhism. This is the inevitable trend of the times, because Humanistic Buddhism is the Buddhism needed by the people.

ENDNOTES AND GLOSSARY

Endnotes:

[1] *Eastern Han Dynasty*: Also known as the "Latter Han Dynasty" (25-220 C.E.). According to Chinese Buddhist history, Buddhism was transmitted into China during the reign of Emperor Ming (59-75 C.E.).

[2] *the right Dharma*: Indicating the Buddha's teachings, which lead to liberation.

[3] *Lianchi*: Also known as "Zhuhong" (1532-1612 C.E.); one of four great masters during the Ming Dynasty, he stressed the teachings of the Pure Land School.

[4] *Ming Dynasty*: It lasted from 1368 to 1644 C.E. Compared with other Chinese dynasties, Buddhism declined during the Ming, but there were still some great masters to inherit the Dharma transmission, like Lianchi, Zhenke, Ouyi, and Hanshan.

[5] *Ouyi*: Or "Ouyi Zhixu" (1599-1655 C.E.). Because he resided in Lingfeng late in his life, he was also called "Lingfeng Ouyi." In teaching, he claimed to integrate the doctrines of the Pure Land, Chan, and Vinaya Schools. Regarding practice, he emphasized the recitation of the Buddhas' names. He also stressed the integration of the teachings of Buddhism, Confucianism, and Daoism.

[6] *the Period of the Republic of China*: From 1911 C.E. to present; the Republic of China was founded by Dr. Sun Yat-sen.

[7] *Mt. Wutai*: Literally, "Five-Terrace Mountains," it is one of the four most famous mountains in China and a very important pilgrimage site for Chinese Buddhists who venerate the Bodhisattva Manjusri (Wenshu).

[8] *Daoming*: A Chan master during the Tang Dynasty; also known as "Muzhou Daoming" (780-877 C.E.). He belonged to the Dharma lineage of Chan Master Huangbo Xiyun.

[9] *Shibei*: A Chan master at the end of the Tang Dynasty; a Dharma brother of Chan Master Xuefeng Yicun.

[10] *Daopi*: A master (889-955 C.E.) who lived toward the end of the Tang Dynasty in China.

[11] *novice*: A monastic who has not yet received full ordination (see Sramanera or Sramaneri in the glossary).

[12] *Dongshan Liangjie*: The founder of the Caodong School of Chinese Chan Buddhism (807-869 C.E.). He was tonsured by Lingmo, and studied the Dharma under the instruction of Chan Masters Nanquan Puyuan, Guishan Lingyou, and Yunyan Tansheng.

[13] *Jin Dynasty*: The dynasty from 265 to 420 C.E., which is divided into two periods: the Western Jin and the Eastern Jin. During this time, Buddhism flourished in China, and many famous translators and commentators appeared. For example, Dharmaraksa and Kumarajiva came to China from India and translated many important Buddhist scriptures; Daoan wrote many works to explain and interpret the sutras.

[14] *Fakuang*: Also known as "Zhu Fakuang," he was a master during the Eastern Jin Dynasty. He spent most of his life in residence on the western side of Mt. Tianmu teaching the Dharma; his teachings stressed the doctrines of the *Lotus Sutra*.

[15] *Yuan Dynasty*: The period from 1264 to 1367 C.E., during which China was ruled by a foreign ethnic group, the Mongolians, for the first time. During this time, Buddhism was respected and endorsed by the emperors, and Lamaism (Tibetan Buddhism) became the national religion in China.

[16] *Yinjian*: A Chan master (1202-1257 C.E.) of the Linji School who lived toward the end of the Song Dynasty; also named "Master Fori Yuanming." He was tonsured by Zhong'guan Zhaogong at age eleven in 1212 C.E., and was fully ordained under the Zhaogong lineage.

[17] *Niaoke*: A Chan master (741-824 C.E.) of the Niutou School during the Tang Dynasty; also known as "Niaoke Daolin."

[18] *Song Dynasty*: The dynasty from 960 to 1278 C.E., which is divided

into two periods: the Northern Song and the Southern Song. During this time, Buddhism experienced a period of consolidation of the schools. In addition, some features of Confucianism and Daoism were integrated with Buddhism, giving Chinese Buddhism its unique characteristics.

[19] *Zhenjing Kewen*: A Chan master (1025-1102 C.E.) during the Northern Song Dynasty; also known as "Yunan Kewen." He studied the Dharma under Chan Master Huanglong Huinan. His teachings were compiled in the *Sayings of Yunan Kewen*.

[20] *Book of Rites* [*Da Dai Liji*]: It was collected and edited by Dai De during the Western Han Dynasty.

[21] *Zhou Dunyi*: A philosopher and poet (1017-1073 C.E.) during the Northern Song Dynasty. He came to be known as the "founding ancestor" of the Cheng-Zhu School of Neo-Confucianism. He wrote the *Illustrated Explanation of the Supreme Polarity* [*Taiji Tu*].

[22] *six sense organs*: Referring to the eyes, ears, nose, tongue, body, and mind.

[23] *Mingjiao Qisong*: A Chan master of the Yunmen School during the Song Dynasty (1007-1072 C.E.). He studied the Dharma under Chan Master Dongshan Xiaocong. He emphasized two notions: the equal importance of studying doctrines and practicing Chan, and that there are commonalities between Buddhism and Confucianism.

[24] *tyrants Jie, Zhou, Li, and You*: Jie was the last emperor of the Xia Dynasty, reigning from 1818 to 1766 B.C.E. Zhou was the last emperor of the Shang Dynasty, reigning from 1154 to 1122 B.C.E. Li and You were both emperors during the Zhou Dynasty. Li reigned from 878 to 827 B.C.E.; You reigned from 781 to 770 B.C.E.

[25] *Boyi or Shuqi*: Two ancient Chinese mythical legendary figures (around the end of the Shang Dynasty and early Zhou Dynasty). They were ancient paragons of virtue, who chose to starve themselves to death in the mountains rather than make even the slightest

compromise in their ideals and moral values.

26 *Fenyang Wude*: Also known as "Fenyang Shanzhao" (947-1024 C.E.); a Chan master of the Linji School during the Song Dynasty. He studied the Dharma under Chan Master Shengnian; his teachings were compiled in the *Sayings of Chan Master Fenyang Wude.*

27 *dhuta*: "Dhuta" is a Sanskrit term, which literally means to cultivate the body and mind, and to eliminate greedy desires. "A dhuta" refers to one who diligently cultivates oneself and practices asceticism.

28 *Damei Fachang*: A Chan master during the Tang Dynasty (752-839 C.E.); he studied the Dharma under the instruction of Master Mazu Daoyi.

29 *the Sixth Patriarch*: Referring to the Chan Master Huineng (638-713 C.E.).

30 *Du Fu*: A famous poet (712-770 C.E.) during the Tang Dynasty. In the history of Chinese literature, he rivaled Li Bai in fame and status, and was given the title "the saint of poetry" by subsequent generations.

31 *Loving-kindness, compassion, joy, and equanimity*: Known as "the four immeasurable states of mind."

32 *Matangi*: After she became a disciple of the Buddha, she diligently cultivated herself and eventually attained arhatship.

33 *Utpalavarna (Lotus Blossom Girl)*: One of the Buddha's female disciples; the foremost in the supernatural power of psychic traveling among the bhiksunis.

34 *arana-samadhi*: The word "arana" literally means no dispute. When attaining the state of arana-samadhi, one has no dispute or distinction between oneself and others because one has already realized the truth of emptiness.

35 *Emperor Huizong and Emperor Qinzong*: The last two emperors during the Northern Song Dynasty; their reigns were from 1101 to 1126 C.E.

36 the upheaval of Jingkang: In 1126 C.E., the Jin army came to the capital Bianjing of the Northern Song Dynasty and kidnapped the Emperors Huizong and Qinzong, which led to the collapse of the Northern Song Dynasty.

37 *Fadao*: (1084-1147 C.E.) During the reign of Emperor Gaozong, he completed the *Brief Instruction of the Monastic History in the Great Song Dynasty.*

38 *An Lushan Rebellion*: (755-763 C.E.) An Lushan was a non-Chinese general appointed by Tang Emperor Xuanzong (r.712-756 C.E.). He became extremely powerful and amassed a large army, which he used in 755 C.E. to rebel against the Tang court. The war lasted for eight years and was extremely destructive, which led to the beginning of the decline of the Tang Dynasty.

39 *Tang Dynasty*: (618-907 C.E.) One of the most important, brilliant periods in Chinese cultural history and considered one of the greatest eras of Chinese civilization in both religion and the arts, the Tang is considered the golden age of Chinese Buddhism. During this period, Buddhism flourished and became the national religion. Many great achievements occurred during this era, most notably the translation of the sutras. For example, in 629 C.E., Xuanzang began his pilgrimage from China to India, where he spent over ten years (until 645 C.E.) studying original Buddhist texts and gathering hundreds of Buddhist records and writings before returning to China. Because of noted Buddhist travelers like Xuanzang, Buddhism quickly spread throughout China and influenced many areas of Chinese life, including language, literature, philosophy, art, and architecture.

40 *Shenhui*: A Chan master (668-760 C.E.); the founder of the Heze School and a student of Chan Master Huineng.

41 *Zongyang*: An active monastic in the late 19th century and early 20th century (1865-1921 C.E.). At the age of sixteen, he was tonsured by Master Yaokan. During his lifetime, he was active in political reform and participated in the activities led by Dr. Sun Yat-Sen. He

was the chief editor of *Su Newspaper* and contributed greatly in the printing of the *Pinqie Buddhist Canon,* a Buddhist Canon consisting of 8,416 fascicles.

42 *Qixia Temple*: Located in Nanjing, Jiangsu Province; one of the four great monasteries in Chinese Buddhism.

43 *Trayastrimasa Heaven*: Pali, Tavatimsa; also known as the "Thirty-Three Heaven," located on the top of Mt. Sumeru according to Buddhist cosmology.

44 *the Sakya clan*: Referring to the tribe to which Sakyamuni Buddha belonged.

45 *the past seven lives*: Implying innumerable previous lives.

46 *three bonds in human relations*: Indicating the relationships of emperor and minister, father and son (parents and children), and husband and wife.

47 *Elder Sudatta*: The word "Sudatta" means "well-giving." Elder Sudatta was an elder of the city Sravasti, and an administrator for King Prasenajit. He was also known as "Anathapindana." After taking refuge in the Buddha, he built the Jetavana Grove (see Jetavana in the glossary) as a place for the Buddha to give discourses on the Dharma and for the Sangha to gather.

48 *non-humans, ghosts, and mara*: Non-humans refers to asuras, the beings in hell, or the realm of hungry ghosts; mara refers to the devil or demon.

49 *the ninety-eight worries*: In Buddhism, afflictions can be categorized into ninety-eight categories.

50 *Zhizhe*: Or "Tiantai Zhiyi," which literally means "the wise" (538-597 C.E.); the founder of the Tiantai (Tientai) School of Chinese Buddhism, he was also known as the Great Master of Tiantai. His many works include *Great Techniques of Stopping [Delusion] and Seeing [Truth]*, *Profound Meanings of the Lotus Sutra [Fahua Jing Xuan Yi]*, and *Explanations on the Passages and Sentences of the Lotus Sutra [Fahua Wen Ju]*. Together, these three are known as

"the three great works of the Tiantai School."

51 *eighty-four thousand Dharma methods*: Implying all the teachings taught by the Buddha.

52 *Hanshan Deqing*: A Chan master (1546-1623 C.E.) during the Ming Dynasty; one of four great Chan Masters at the end of the Ming Dynasty. He claimed that practitioners needed to cultivate themselves by reciting the Buddhas' names and contemplating on "koans."

53 *mani pearl*: The word "mani" means pearl or gem; in Buddhism, it can eliminate disasters and diseases, and purify water.

54 *the three Daoist masters of the Grass Hut*: According to Chinese legends, there were three brothers, named Ying, Gu, and Zhong. Ying, the oldest brother, renounced on Mt. Mao (Grass Hut) at the age of eighteen and practiced Daoism. Later, his younger brothers, Gu and Zhong, both abandoned their official positions and went to Mt. Mao, also to practice Daoism, which is why they were later known as "the three Daoist masters of the Grass Hut."

55 *Guishan Lingyou*: A Chan master (771-853 C.E.) during the Tang Dynasty; founder of the Guiyang School of Chan Buddhism.

56 *Zhishun*: A Chan master during the Tang Dynasty. He gave teachings on the Dharma and explained the *Sutra on Contemplation of the Buddha of Infinite Life [Amitayurdhyana Sutra]* on Mt. Lu.

57 *Twenty-Six Books of History*: Ch. *Ershiliu Shi*; twenty-six historical books, which recorded Chinese history from the Age of the Five Rulers (2853-2255 B.C.E.) to the Qing Dynasty (1644-1908 C.E.).

58 *Emperor Wu of the Liang Dynasty*: (464-549 C.E.) He was an important patron of Buddhism. Initially, Emperor Wu believed in Daoism, but later became a devout Buddhist and took the bodhisattva precepts himself. He also compiled *The Repentance of the Emperor Wu of Liang* to deliver the deceased Empress Xi from suffering in the animal realm. This repentance text has been passed down to the present time.

59 *Daoism*: A Chinese philosophical and religious system, Daoism was founded by Laozi (604-531 B.C.E.) in the 6th century B.C.E. His teachings were passed down orally before they were compiled in the third century B.C.E. in a book called *Dao De Jing*.

60 *Lu Mengzheng*: A prime minister during the reigns of the Emperors Taizong and Zhenzong, during the Northern Song Dynasty.

61 *Han Yu*: An eminent literary figure (768-824 C.E.), he took it upon himself to weaken the influence of Buddhism in order to restore Confucianism. He was also one of the leaders in the Confucian counterattack on Buddhism. In his late years, his beliefs changed and he became a devout Buddhist.

62 *Ouyang Xiu*: A famous literary scholar and historian (1007-1072 C.E.) during the Northern Song Dynasty, he was also one of the eight literary masters of the Tang and Song Dynasties.

63 *Daokai*: A Chan master (1043-1118 C.E.) during the Song Dynasty, he belonged to the Dharma lineage of the Caodong School; also known as "Furong Daokai."

64 *Daoyuan*: The founder of the Soto School of Zen Buddhism in Japan (1200-1253 C.E.).

65 *Qing Dynasty*: From 1644 to 1912 C.E., this dynasty was the outcome of a successful invasion by the Manchus, the second foreign ethnic group to rule the whole of China. During this dynasty, all emperors believed in Lamaism (Tibetan Buddhism).

66 *Taixu*: Usually known as "Tai-hsu" (1889-1947C.E.), he was a reformer of Chinese Buddhism in the late 19th and early 20th century. His works are included in the *Complete Works of Taixu* [*Taixu Dashi Quan Shu*].

67 *Yuan Liaofan*: Originally named Yuan Xuehai (1533-1606 C.E.), he was a famous Confucian scholar during the Ming Dynasty. When he reached middle age, he went to Mt. Qixia and met Chan Master Yungu Hui. Then he became a devout Buddhist and diligently practiced the Dharma. His book *Liao Fan's Four Lessons* has been read

widely by Chinese families since the Ming and Qing Dynasties and into the present day. This work has also had long-lasting and profound influence on Japan's political and economic administrations.

68 *pattra-leaf sutras*: The earliest version of Buddhist sutras; they were written on pattra leaf, and can be traced back to ancient India.

69 *Fazhen*: Toward the end of the Yuan Dynasty, the Buddhist sutras and scriptures were incomplete; for this reason, Fazhen made a great vow to reprint the Buddhist Canon. She spent thirty years completing this work, known as the *Jinke Buddhist Canon* in Chinese Buddhism.

70 *Zhuhong*: Same as Master Lianchi (see endnote 3).

71 *Su Dongpo*: Also called Su Shi (1036-1101CE), he was one of the most famous scholars during the Tang and Song Dynasties. He was famous for his poetry, calligraphy, and painting. He was also an avid student of Buddhist teachings, which he often discussed with his good friend, Chan Master Foyin. With regard to his practice, he stressed both Pure Land and Chan methods.

72 *Foyin*: Also known as "Foyin Liaoyuan" (1032-1098 C.E.), he was a famous master during the Song Dynasty and studied the Dharma under Chan Master Yuantong Juna's instruction. He was a good friend of contemporary scholars of the time, such as Su Dongpo and Huang Shangu.

73 *Bai Juyi*: A famous poet (772-846 C.E.) during the Tang Dynasty. He was a Confucian scholar, but at middle age, he began to study Buddhism and later became close to many great masters. He practiced Chan.

74 *Mingjiao*: Same as Mingjiao Qisong (see endnote 29).

75 *Yungu Hui*: Also known as "Yungu Fahui" (1500-1579 C.E.), he was a master during the Ming Dynasty and was the teacher of Chan Masters Hanshan Deqing and Yuan Liaofan.

76 *Dadian*: Also known as "Dadian Baotong" (732-824 C.E.), he was a Chan master during the Tang Dynasty. He was Chan Master Yaoshan

Weiyan's Dharma brother, and belonged to the Dharma lineage of Chan Master Shitou Xiqian.

77 *Yuantong Na*: Also known as "Yuantong Juna" (1010-1071 C.E.), he was a Chan master of the Yunmen School during the Song Dynasty. Because he resided in the Yuantong Monastery in his late years, he was also known as "Yuantong Na."

78 *Pure Land of Ultimate Bliss*: Referring to the Western Pure Land, which was established by the power of Amitabha Buddha's forty-eight great vows.

79 *Zhou Rites [Zhou Li]*: One of the Confucian classics. It functioned as the constitution during the Zhou Dynasty (909-255 B.C.E.), encompassing politics, the economy, the military, diplomacy, and law.

80 *Dazhu Huihai*: A Chan master during the Tang Dynasty and a student of Chan Master Mazu Daoyi.

81 *Yaoshan Weiyan*: A Chan master (751-834 C.E.) belonging to the Dharma lineage of Chan Master Qingyuan Xingsi; also a student of Chan Masters Shitou Xiqian and Mazu Daoyi.

82 *Nanyang Huizhong*: A Chan master (?-775 C.E.) during the Tang Dynasty; appointed as the Imperial Master during the reigns of Emperors Xuanzong, Suzong, and Daizong. He was also a student of Chan Master Huineng.

83 *Fazang Xianshou*: A master (643-712 C.E.) during the Tang Dynasty; the Third Patriarch of the Huayan School.

84 *Qingliang Cheng'guan*: A master (738-839 C.E.) during the Tang Dynasty; the Fourth Patriarch of the Huayan School, he was appointed as the Imperial Master during the reign of Emperor Shunzong.

85 *Wuda Zhixuan*: A master (811-883 C.E.) during the Tang Dynasty; he was appointed as the Imperial Master during the reigns of Emperor Xuanzong, Yizong, and Xizong.

86 *Yulin Tongxiu*: A Chan master (1614 - 1675 C.E.) during the Qing Dynasty, he belonged to the Dharma lineage of the Linji School and

was appointed as the Imperial Master during the reign of Emperor Shizu.

87 *Tiantai Zhiyi*: Also known as "Zhizhe" (see endnote 55).

88 *Emperor Taizong of the Tang Dynasty*: Also known as "Li Shiming" (598-649 C.E.); considered to be one of the greatest Chinese emperors. During his reign, Buddhism was strongly supported by the national government and quickly flourished throughout the entire nation. Because of his support, the mission of translating sutras could be completed under the leadership of Master Xuanzong, which established a solid foundation for Buddhism in China. His reign, known as the Prosperity of Zhenguan, was outstanding as an era of peace and prosperity; one of the most flourishing periods during the Tang Dynasty.

89 *Yao Guangxiao*: In 1404 C.E., Emperor Chengzu of the Ming Dynasty ordered Master Daoyan to return to secular life and gave him the name "Guangxiao." He wrote *Daoyu Lu*.

90 *Emperor Yongle*: Also known as Emperor Chengzu; he reigned from 1403 to 1424 C.E.

91 *Varsakara*: An important administrator for King Ajatasatru in the Maghada Kingdom. He contributed greatly to building the city Pataliputra.

92 *Emperor Gaozong of the Southern Song*: His reign was from 1127 to 1163 C.E. Because of the upheaval of Jingkang, he moved the capital to the South, which marked the beginning of the Southern Song Dynasty in Chinese history.

93 *Liu Bingzhong*: (1216-1274 C.E.) Before returning to secular life, his Dharma name was "Zicong."

94 *Han Chinese*: Han is the major ethnic group in China; generally the people living in the Central Plains.

95 *Daoan*: A major Buddhist figure during the Eastern Jin Dynasty (312-385 C.E.). He made major contributions to the editing and translating of the Buddhist Canon. He also encouraged the Emperor Fu Jian

to invite Kumarajiva to come to China and translate the Buddhist Canon.

96 *Emperor Yao Xing*: (366-416 C.E.) The length of his reign was around twenty-two years.

97 *Ximing Pavilion*: Located in Changan. In 401 C.E., Yao Xing invited Kumarajuva to reside there.

98 *supernatural power*: That which is beyond or above the natural, or cannot be controlled by natural law. In Buddhism, there are six kinds: the supernatural powers of psychic traveling, clairaudience (deva-ear), clairvoyance (deva-eye), mental telepathy, knowledge of past and future, and ending contamination.

99 *Pure Land of the Medicine Buddha*: Also known as the Eastern Pure Land, or the Land of Pure Crystal, which was established by the power of Medicine Buddha's twelve great vows.

Buddhist Terms and Names:

Ajatasatru: He was the king of Magadha Kingdom during the Buddha's time, and killed his father, King Bimbisara, in order to inherit the throne. Later, he repented his wrongdoings and became a follower of the Buddha.

Alaya consciousness: Indicating the eighth consciousness, also known as the "store consciousness" in the Mind-Only School.

Ananda: One of the ten great disciples of the Buddha. He is noted as the foremost in hearing and learning. After the Buddha entered parinirvana, Ananda is said to have compiled the sutras in Vaibhara Cave, which is in Magadha, India, where the five hundred disciples of the Buddha were assembled.

Aryadeva: Also known as Kana-deva. Born in the third century in Southern India, he was a student of Nagarjuna. He had a thorough understanding of the teachings of the Madhyamika School and was the author of the *Treatise of a Hundred Verses* [*Satasastra*].

Asanga: He founded the Yogacara School of Buddhism along with his brother, Vasubandhu. He lived in 4th century C.E.

Asceticism: Skt. "dhuta"; which means to eliminate afflictions and sufferings, to cultivate the purification of the mind and the body, and to abandon greedy desires.

Asvaghosa: The Twelfth Patriarch of the Dharma transmission in Buddhism (100-160 C.E.); a famous Buddhist poet with many well-known works including the *Buddhacarita* and the *Treatise on the Awakening of Faith in Mahayana*.

Avalokitesvara: Literally, "He who hears the sounds of the world." In Mahayana Buddhism, Avalokitesvara is known as the Bodhisattva of Compassion. He can manifest himself in any form necessary in order to help any being. He is considered one of the great bodhisattvas in Mahayana Buddhism. In China, he is usually portrayed in female form and is known as "Guan Yin."

Bhiksu: The male members of the Buddhist sangha, who have renounced household life and received full ordination. According to the *Treatise on Perfection of Great Wisdom*, the word "bhiksu" can be traced back literally to the words "bhiks" (begging) and "bhinna-klesa" (eliminating afflictions). Therefore, bhiksus are also known as beggars or the ones who eliminate afflictions.

Bhiksuni: The female members of the Buddhist sangha who have renounced household life and received full ordination.

Bimbisara: One of the kings of Magadha Kingdom during the Buddha's time. He was the father of King Ajatasatru, who killed Bimbasara to inherit the throne. King Bimbisara and his queen, Vedehi, both had deep faith in Buddhism and were devout followers of the Buddha. After the Buddha's enlightenment, the King often invited the Buddha to the city of Rajagrha to teach the Dharma. The king also built many places for the gathering of the sangha. As a result, his kingdom was a well-known, active area for Buddhism.

Bodhi: It means enlightenment. In the state of enlightenment, one is awakened to the true nature of self; one is enlightened to one's own Buddha Nature. Such a person has already eliminated all afflictions and delusions, and achieved prajna-wisdom.

Bodhi mind: Skt. "bodhicitta." The mind that seeks enlightenment.

Bodhisattva path: Skt. "Bodhisattva-carya"; indicating the cultivation of the bodhisattvas in Mahayana Buddhism. The main philosophy of the bodhisattva path is to attain Buddhahood and liberate all sentient beings through the practice of the six perfections.

Buddha: Literally, "awakened one." When "the Buddha" is used, it usually refers to the historical Buddha, Sakyamuni Buddha.

Buddha Nature: The inherent nature that exists in all beings. It is the capability to achieve Buddhahood.

Buddhahood: The attainment and expression that characterizes a Buddha. Buddhahood is the goal of all beings.

Buddhism: Founded by Sakyamuni Buddha around 2,500 years ago. Its basic doctrines include the Three Dharma Seals, the Four Noble Truths, the Noble Eightfold Path, the Twelve Links of Dependent Origination, the six perfections, and the concepts of impermanence and emptiness. Its main three traditions are the Mahayana, Theravada, and Vajrayana. While Buddhism has been a popular religion in South, Central, and East Asia, it is currently gaining popularity in the West.

Causes and conditions: Referring to the primary cause (causes) and the secondary causes (conditions). The seed out of which a plant or a flower grows is a good illustration of a primary cause; the elements of soil, humidity, sunlight, and so forth, could be considered secondary causes.

Chan: The form of the Chinese transliteration of the Sanskrit term, dhyana; it refers to meditative concentration.

Chan School: One school of Chinese Buddhism. It was founded by Bodhidharma, emphasizes the cultivation of intrinsic wisdom, and teaches that enlightenment is clarifying the mind and seeing one's own true nature. Another major tenant of the Chan School is that the Dharma is wordlessly transmitted from mind to mind.

Confucianism: The philosophy named after Confucius (551-479 B.C.E.), who is known as "Kung Tzu" in Chinese and was an early Chinese moral philosopher. It was the official philosophy of China, established in 3rd century B.C.E.

Cycle of birth and death: Skt. "samsara" or "jatimarana." Also known as transmigration. When sentient beings die, they are reborn into one of the six realms of existence (the realms of heaven, human, asura, animals, hungry ghost, and hell). The cycle is continuous and endless due to the karmic result of one's deeds.

Dependent origination: The central principle that phenomena do not come into existence independently but only as a result of causes and conditions; thus, no phenomena possesses an independent self-nature. This concept is also referred to as interdependence. The twelve factors of dependent origination are: ignorance, karma, formation of consciousness, mind and body, the six senses, contact, feeling, craving, grasping, becoming, birth, and aging and death.

Dharma: When capitalized, it means: 1) the ultimate truth and 2) the teachings of the Buddha. When the Dharma is applied or practiced in life it is referred to as: 3) righteousness or virtues. When it appears with a lowercase "d": 4) anything that can be thought of, experienced, or named; close in meaning to "phenomena."

Dharma-body: Skt. "Dharmakaya." Indicating the true nature of a Buddha, also referring to the absolute Dharma that the Buddha attained. It is also one of three bodies possessed by a Buddha.

Dharma realms: Skt. "dharma-dhatu." It indicates the notion of true nature that encompasses all phenomena. As a space or realm of dharmas, it is the uncaused and immutable totality in which all phenomena arise, abide, and extinguish.

Dharmodgata: Also known as "Fayong"; a traveling monk during the Tang Dynasty, who diligently practiced asceticism and made pilgrimages to Kucina, Kasmira, Kusana, and India. After the pilgrimages, he returned to China and translated sutras.

Dr. Sun Yat-sen: The father of the Republic of China (1911-present).

Emptiness: Skt. "sunya." A basic concept in Buddhism. It means that everything existing in the world is due to dependent origination and has no permanent self or substance. It can be basically categorized into two groups: 1) emptiness of people (living beings), which means that human beings or other living beings have no unchanging, substantial self; and 2) emptiness of dharmas, which means that existence of all phenomena are due to causes and conditions.

Enlightenment: The state of awakening to the Truth—freedom from all afflictions and sufferings.

Early Buddhism: Named for the specific period of Buddhism from the time when Sakyamuni Buddha established the Sangha to 100-200 years after his parinirvana. During that period, Buddhism in India had not yet been divided into the eighteen schools.

Five contemplations: Five methods of contemplation for stopping and eliminating delusions: 1) contemplation on the impurity of the body (Skt. asubha-smrti), which enables sentient beings to eliminate greed in the mind; 2) contemplation on compassion (Skt. maritri-smrti), which enables sentient beings to eliminate anger and hatred in the mind; 3) contemplation on dependent origination (Skt. idampratyay-ata-pratiyasamutpadasmrti), which enables sentient beings to eliminate ignorance and afflictions in the mind; and 4) contemplation on a Buddha's name (Skt. buddhanusmrti), which enables sentient beings to eliminate unwholesome thoughts and the stress of uncomfortable situations. Sometimes this fourth method is replaced by "Contemplation on the worlds" (Skt. dhatu-prabheda-smrti), also known as contemplation on analysis or non-self, which is based on the concept that all phenomena are made up of the elements of earth, fire, water, wind, consciousness, and emptiness. This form of contemplation helps sentient beings to eliminate their attachment to self. The last contemplation is: 5) Contemplation on breathing (Skt. anapana-smrti), which helps sentient beings to eliminate distracted states of mind and achieve one-pointedness of mind.

Five great violations: They are patricide, matricide, killing an arhat, shedding the blood of a Buddha, and destroying the harmony of the sangha.

Five precepts: The principles of conduct and discipline that were established by the Buddha for wholesome and harmonious living. They are: 1) do not kill; 2) do not steal; 3) do not engage in sexual misconduct; 4) do not lie; and 5) do not take intoxicants.

Five vehicles: Indicates the vehicles of human (manusyayana), heaven (deva-yana), sravaka, pratyeka-buddha, and bodhisattva.

Fo Guang Shan: The monastic order established by Venerable Master Hsing Yun in 1967 in Kaoshiung, Taiwan.

Four elements: Skt. "catvari mahabhutani." In Buddhism, all matters in the world are composed of the elements of earth (prthivi-dhatu), water (ab-dhatu), fire (tejo-dhatu), and wind (vayu-dhatu).

Four great kindnesses: Indicating great kindnesses of: 1) parents; 2) sentient beings; 3) rulers and nations; and 4) the Triple Gem.

Four immeasurable states of mind: Skt. "catvary apramanani." 1) The state of boundless loving-kindness (maitry-apramana); to give others happiness. 2) The state of boundless compassion (karunapramana); to help others away from suffering. 3) The state of boundless joy (muditapramana); to feel joyful when others can stay away from suffering. 4) The state of boundless equanimity (upeksapramana); to treat others equally without discrimination.

Four means of embracing: Skt. "catvari-samgraha-vastuni." The four methods that bodhisattvas use to guide sentient beings to the path of liberation: 1) giving (dana-samgraha); 2) kind words (priya-vadita-samgraha); 3) altruism and beneficence (artha-carya-samgraha); and 4) sympathy and empathy (samanarthata-samgraha).

Four Noble Truths: A foundation and essential teaching of Buddhism that describes the presence of suffering, the cause of suffering, the path leading to the cessation of suffering, and the cessation of suffering. The Four Truths are: 1) in existence, there is suffering; 2) the causes of suffering are greed, anger, and ignorance; 3) it is possible for suffering to cease (e.g., the cessation of suffering); and 4) the way leading to the cessation of the suffering is the Noble Eightfold Path and other teachings of the Buddha.

Gatha: Verses.

Great Compassion Dharani: Skt. "Mahakarunikacitta-dharani." This dharani has many different translated versions and lengths, but regardless of the version, it is basically known as the dharani of merits and virtues of Avalokitesvara's attainment. According to the sutras, sincerely reciting this dharani 108 times can eliminate unwholesome karmas and purify the body and mind.

Hinayana Buddhism: Also known as the "Small Vehicle" or "Lesser Vehicle." Literally, it means the vehicle that can only carry a few people. This term is used to refer to one who only focuses on self-cultivation.

Humanistic Buddhism: The primary teaching of Venerable Master Hsing Yun; its philosophy emphasizes practicing Buddhism in daily life and building a pure land in our living world.

Impermanence: One of the most basic truths taught by the Buddha. It is the concept that all conditioned dharmas, or phenomena, will arise, abide, change, and disappear due to causes and conditions.

Jetavana: Or known as Jetavana Grove; located in the south of the city of Sravasti in the Uttara-Kosala Kingdom. It was donated by the Elder Sudatta to the Buddha for discoursing the Dharma and the gathering of the Sangha. Since the Buddha discoursed the Dharma there several times, Jetavana Grove is a famous historical site for Buddhists.

Kalpa: The measuring unit of time in ancient India; a kalpa is an immense and inconceivable length of time. Buddhism adapts it to refer to the period of time between the creation and re-creation of the worlds.

Kaniska: The third king of Kusana (or Kushan) Kingdom; his reign is dated around the 1st century C.E. The period of his reign is considered an important time of political and cultural history in ancient India. According to the Buddhist teachings, he was the other great king besides King Asoka and was converted by Asvanghosa. Toward the end of his reign (about 100 C.E.), Kaniska assembled Parsva, Vasumitra, Dharmatrata, Buddhadeva, and 496 other monastics to establish the Third Council, which is also known as the Council of Kaniska in Buddhist history.

Karma: This means "work, action, or deeds" and is related to the Law of Cause and Effect. All deeds, whether good or bad, produce effects. The effects may be experienced instantly, or they may not come into fruition for many years or even many lifetimes.

Kasyapa-matanga: One of the monastics known for spreading Buddhism into China (?-73 C.E.). In 67 C.E., he and Zhu Falan were invited by Emperor Ming of the Eastern Han Dynasty to Luoyang from India. When they brought Buddhist sutras and statues to China, the Emperor built the Baima (White Horse) Temple for them. They stayed there and translated the first Chinese Buddhist sutra–the *Sutra of Forty-two*

Sections.

King Asoka: He reigned as the King of the Maurya Kingdom in India from 272-236 B.C.E. He was the foremost royal patron of Buddhism in India and the first monarch to rule over a united India.

King Prasenajit: A king of the Kausala Kingdom during the Buddha's time. He also ruled over the Kasi Kingdom and was a devout follower of the Buddha.

King Virudhaka: One of the Four Heavenly Kings; believed to have lived in the south of Mt. Sumeru, and also known as the "guardian god" in Buddhism.

Law of Cause and Effect: Skt. "hetu-phala." This is the most basic doctrine in Buddhism, which explains the formation of all relations and connections in the world. This law means that the arising of each and every phenomenon is due to its own causes and conditions, and the actual form, or appearance, of all phenomena is the effect.

Liberation: Skt. "vimoksa"; which means free from all afflictions, sufferings, and the cycle of birth and death.

Magadha: One of sixteen great kingdoms during the period when the Buddha was present in this world. Its location is around the present day Bihar. This kingdom was also one of the active areas of Buddhism, especially during the reigns following that of King Bimbisara. The cities of Patna, Bodhigaya and Rajagrha were all places within the kingdom where the Buddha discoursed the Dharma and the Sangha gathered.

Mahakasyapa: One of the ten great disciples of the Buddha. He is known as foremost in the practice of asceticism and was regarded as the chief of the order. In Chan, he is considered the First Patriarch of Dharma Transmission, because of his smiling and becoming enlightened when Sakyamuni Buddha held up a flower.

Mahaprajapati: Prince Siddhartha's aunt who raised him after his mother died. She later became a female disciple of Sakyamuni Buddha. The bhiksuni order was established as a result of her request to the Buddha for renunciation.

Mahayana Buddhism: Mahayana, literally means "Great Vehicle." One of the two main traditions of Buddhism, Theravada being the other one. Mahayana Buddhism stresses that helping other sentient beings to achieve enlightenment is as important as self-liberation.

Maitreya Bodhisattva: The future Buddha. It is said that he currently presides over Tusita Heaven, where he is expounding the Dharma to heavenly beings in the inner palace.

Maudgalyayana: One of the Buddha's ten great disciples; also known as "Mahamaudgalyayana" or "Moggallana" in Pali. He is known to be foremost in supernatural powers.

Middle Way: A teaching of Sakyamuni Buddha, which teaches the avoidance of all extremes.

Milinda: Also known as Menandros. In Indian history, he was a particularly important king. He invaded India and ruled an area extending from central India to Afghanistan from approximately 200 to 100 B.C.E. His great contribution included integrating Greek and Indian cultures. He also had a good relationship with Buddhism. He was most well-known for his discussions and debates with Bhiksu Nagasena, after which he was converted to Buddhism.

Mt. Sumeru: Or Mt. Meru; according to Buddhist cosmology, it is the center of our world.

Nagarjuna: Born in Southern India in the 2nd or 3rd century. He is the founder of the Madhyamika School (the Middle School) and the author of many commentaries and treatises. His famous works include *Treatise on the Perfection of Great Wisdom*, *Treatise on the Middle Path*, the *Merits of Right Deeds Sutra*, and many more. Therefore, he was given the title "Master of a Thousand Commentaries." He is a very important philosopher in Buddhism.

Namo: Skt. "Namas." It means "to submit oneself to" or "to take refuge in."

Nirvana: Pali, "nibbana." The original meaning of this word is "extinguished, calmed, quieted, tamed, or dead." In Buddhism, it refers to the absolute extinction of individual existence, or of all afflictions and desires; it is the state of liberation, beyond birth and death. It is also the final goal in Buddhism.

Noble Eightfold Path: Skt. "astanga-marga-hamani"; eight right ways leading to liberation. They are: 1) right view (samyga-drsti); 2) right thought (samyak-samkalpa); 3) right speech (samyga-vac); 4) right action (samyak-karmanta); 5) right livelihood (samyag-ajiva); 6) right effort (samyag-vyayana); 7) right mindfulness (samyak-smrti); and 8) right concentration (samyak-samadhi).

Non-self: Skt. "anatman" or "niratman"; Pali, "anattan." A basic concept in Buddhism. It means that all phenomena and beings in the world have no real, permanent, and substantial self. Everything arises, abides, changes, and extinguishes based on the law of dependent origination.

Parinirvana: A synonym for "nirvana." It is the state of having completed all merits and perfections and eliminated all unwholesomeness. Usually, it is used to refer to the time when the Buddha physically passed away.

Prajna-wisdom: Prajna-wisdom is the highest form of wisdom. It is the wisdom of insight into the true nature of all phenomena.

Pratyeka-buddhas: Refers to those who awaken to the Truth through their own efforts when they live in a time without a Buddha's presence.

Pure Land: Another term for a Buddha realm, which is established by the vows and cultivation of one who has achieved enlightenment.

Rahula: The son of Prince Siddhartha; one of the Buddha's ten great disciples. At the age of six, he entered the Sangha and was instructed by Sariputra. He was considered foremost in inconspicuous practice.

Sadaparibhuta Bodhisattva: Also known as "the Bodhisattva Never Disparaging." In one of his previous lives, Sakyamuni Buddha was this bodhisattva. According to chapter twenty of the *Lotus Sutra*, he was a bhiksu in the Vinirbhoga Kalpa when the Bhisma-garjitasvararaja Buddha preached the Dharma and always had praise and respect for everyone, including bhiksus, bhiksunis, upasikas, and upasakas, hence his name.

Sakyamuni Buddha: (581-501 B.C.E.) The historical founder of Buddhism. He was born the prince of Kapilavastu, son of King Suddhodana. At the age of twenty-nine, he left the royal palace and his family to search for the meaning of existence. At the age of thirty-five, he attained enlightenment under the Bodhi tree. He then spent the next forty-five years expounding his teachings, which include the Four Noble Truths, the Noble Eightfold Path, the Law of Cause and Effect, and dependent origination. At the age of eighty, he entered the state of parinirvana.

Samadhi: Literally, "establish" or "make firm." It means concentration; a state in which the mind is concentrated in a one-pointed focus and all mental activities are calm. In samadhi, one is free from all distractions, thereby entering a state of inner serenity.

Samsara: Also known as "jatimarana," which means transmigration of birth and death. This refers to when sentient beings die and are then reborn into one of the six realms of existence (the realms of heaven, human, asura, hungry ghost, animal, and hell). This kind of birth and death is continuous and endless, and is due to the karma of unwholesome deeds.

Sangha: Indicating the Buddhist community; in a broad sense it includes both monastics and laypersons. Specifically, it refers to the monastics.

Sariputra: Pali, "Sariputta." One of the Buddha's ten great disciples. He is known as the foremost in wisdom.

Sentient beings: Skt. "sattvas." All beings with consciousness, including celestial beings, asuras, humans, animals, hungry ghosts, and hellish beings. From the Mahayana view, all sentient beings inherently have Buddha Nature and therefore possess the capacity to attain enlightenment.

Siladitya: A king of Kanyakubja Kingdom in central India in the 7th century. According to Buddhist history, he was famous for protecting Buddhism and encouraging Buddhist literature. Among his other great contributions, he was also well-known for his effort to propagate the Dharma after taking refuge in Buddhism, for building numerous stupas, and forming many sanghas (Buddhist communities).

Six dusts: Indicating the six objects reflected by the six bases (sense-organs), which then produce the six consciousnesses.

Six perfections: Also known as the six paramitas. "Paramita" in Sanskrit means "gone to the opposite shore," "transcendent," "complete attainment," "perfection in," and "transcendental virtue," according to the Sanskrit-English Dictionary. The six perfections are: 1) giving charity; 2) upholding precepts; 3) patience; 4) diligence; 5) meditation; and 6) prajna-wisdom.

Six Points of Reverent Harmony Sangha: They are: 1) physical unity by living together; 2) verbal unity by not criticizing others; 3) mental unity through shared joy; 4) moral unity through upholding the same precepts; 5) doctrinal unity in views; and 6) economic unity through sharing.

Sramanera/sramaneraka: Indicating a male novice in a Buddhist order, who has vowed to uphold the ten precepts but has yet to receive full ordination.

Sramaneri/Sramanerika: Indicating a female novice in a Buddhist order, who has vowed to uphold the ten precepts but has yet to receive full ordination.

Subhuti: One of the Buddha's ten great disciples. He was foremost in understanding emptiness.

Suddhodana: The father of Prince Siddhartha, the ruler of Kapilavastu, and the eldest son of Simhahanu. His wife was Queen Maya, but he later married Mahapajapati, the queen's sister following her death.

Suffering: Skt. "duhkha." The First Noble Truth (duhkha-aryasatya); it refers to the state in which the body and mind are oppressed by afflictions.   In Buddhism, it is often categorized into four types–birth, aging, sickness, and death.   An additional four types are sometimes added–separation from loved ones, association with the disliked, inability to obtain what is wanted or desired, and clinging to the five aggregates.

Sutra: Literally, "threaded together." The scriptures directly taught by the Buddha.

Ten wholesome conducts: The ten wholesome actions are: no killing, no stealing, no sexual misconduct, no lying, no duplicity, no harsh words, no flattery, no greed, no anger, and no ignorance.

The Way: Refers to the path leading to liberation taught by the Buddha.

Theravada School: One of the eighteen schools in the Period of Sectarian Buddhism.   In the 3rd century B.C.E., it was transmitted into Sri Lanka from India. Today it is still popular in many areas of South East Asia.

Three Dharma Seals: Also known as the Three Marks of Existence. According to the *Connected Discourses of the Buddha* in the *Chinese Buddhist Canon*, they are: 1) all conditioned dharmas are impermanent (anityah sarva-samskarah); 2) all dharmas are without self (niratmanah saarva-dharmaah); and 3) nirvana is equanimity (santam nirvanam).   In some Buddhist texts such as in the *Dharmapada*, they are: 1) all compounded things are impermanent; 2) all compounded things are unsatisfied; and 3) all dharmas are without self.

Three poisons: Greed, anger, and ignorance.

Three Realms: The realms where sentient beings reside and transmigrate: 1) the realm of sense-desires (kama-dhatu); 2) the realm of form (rupa-dhatu); and 3) the realm of formlessness (arupaya-dhatu).

Three studies: Skt. "tisrah siksah"; Pali, "tisso sikkha."   Including precepts (adhisila), concentration (adhicitta), and wisdom (adhiprajna). Precepts can prevent one from the unwholesomeness of body, speech, and mind.   Concentration can make one eliminate distracting thoughts with a singly focused mind, see the true nature, and attain the path.

Wisdom can enable one to reveal the true nature, eliminate all afflictions, and see the Truth.

Three time periods: Or known as "three periods of time," indicating the
past, the present, and the future.

Tripitaka: The Buddhist Canon known as "Three Baskets." It is divided
into three categories: the sutras (teachings of the Buddha), the vinayas
(precepts and rules), and the abhidharma (commentaries on the
Buddha's teachings).

Triple Gem: Indicating the Buddha, the Dharma, and the Sangha, and also
called the Triple Jewel, or the Three Jewels. The Buddha is the fully
awakened or enlightened one; the Dharma is the teachings imparted
by the Buddha; and the Sangha indicates the community of monastic
members.

Twelve sections of the Buddhist Canon: Skt. "dvadasangabuddha-vacana."
The twelve categories of the Buddha's teachings, classified by format
and content. The twelve categories are: 1) sutra (prose); 2) geya
(verses that correspond to the sutra); 3) vyakarana (originally indicating the explanation of teachings, later referring to the Buddha's
prophecies to his disciples); 4) gatha (verse only); 5) udana (the
Buddha discourses the Dharma, without waiting for someone to make
this request); 6) nidana (describing the causes and conditions of the
Buddha's discourses); 7) avadana (parables); 8) itivrttaka (describing
the stories of the previous lives of the Buddha and his disciples); 9)
jataka (describing the Buddha's practices of great compassion in his
previous lives); 10) vaipula (instructing the profound teachings); 11)
adbhuta-dharma (describing the special events of the Buddha and his
disciples); and 12) upadesa (describing the Buddha's interpretation
about the nature of all dharmas and meanings).

Two vehicles: Indicating the Sravaka and the Pratyeka-buddha.

Udaya a: In the Buddha's time, he was the king of Kausambi Kingdom.
His queen had a deep faith in Buddhism; therefore, he became the

Buddha's follower. According to the *Gradual Discourses of the Buddha*, when the Buddha ascended to heaven and discoursed the Dharma to his mother, the king missed him so much that he ordered the first sculpture of the Buddha's image, hence giving rise to other Buddhist statues.

Upasaka: A layman; a male follower of Buddhism who does not renounce the household life and enter a monastery but who still strives to live a spiritually cultivated life and upholds the teachings and precepts.

Upasika: A female follower of Buddhism who practices the teachings of the Buddha and upholds the precepts.

Vasubandhu: (320-380 C.E.) He founded the Yogacara School of Buddhism, along with his brother, Asanga.

Visakha: Also known as "Mrgara-matr." According to the *Dharmapada*, she was the daughter of an elder in the Anga Kingdom and the wife of Migara. After hearing the Buddha's teachings, she attained the fruit of Stream-Entry, and made eight great vows to make offerings to the monastics.

Vulture Peak: Skt. "Grdhrakuta"; located in the northeast of the city of Rajagrha in Magadha Kingdom. Sakyamuni Buddha discoursed several Mahayana sutras at Vulture Peak including the *Lotus Sutra*. It is now a famous pilgrimage site for Buddhists.

Western Pure Land: The realm where Amitabha Buddha presides. It came into existence due to Amitahba Buddha's forty-eight great vows. Sentient beings can make a vow to be reborn there, where they can practice without obstructions until they attain enlightenment.

Without outflows: Outflows is called "asrava" in Sanskrit and "youlou" in Chinese. Literally, "lou" means leaking, and in Buddhism it represents afflictions. The state of "without outflows" (Skt. "anasrava"; Ch. "wulou") refers to the state of liberation. Sometimes "without outflows" refers to those dharmas free from afflictions and leading to liberation.

Xuanzang: (602-664 C.E.) A great master of the Tang Dynasty. He is one of four great translators in Buddhist history. He studied in India for seventeen years and was responsible for bringing many collections of works, images, pictures, as well as one hundred and fifty relics to China from India. One of his most famous works is the *Buddhist Records of the Western Regions.*

Buddhist Sutras and Other Writings:

A Commentary on the Lotus Sutra [Fahua Yishu]: T: vol. 34, no. 1721; written by Jizang during the Sui Dynasty. Jizang explained the *Lotus Sutra* from the viewpoint of the Sanlun School.

A Record of the Mysterious Significance of Avalokitesvara [Guanyin Xuanyi Ji]: T: vol. 34, no. 1727; spoken by Siming Zhilin during the Song Dynasty, consisting of four fascicles. It is an explanation on the *Mysterious Significance of Avalokitesvara*, written by Master Zhizhe of the Tang Dynasty.

Amitabha Sutra: The *Amitahba Sutra* is one of the three sutras that form the doctrinal basis for the Pure Land School of Mahayana Buddhism.

Biography of Venerable Master Ouyi [Ouyi Dashi Zhuan]: Ouyi (1599-1655 C.E.), also known as Master Lingfeng Ouyi, was a famous master during the Ming Dynasty. At the age of twenty-four, he was tonsured by Master Hanshan and studied under Hanshan's teaching. Master Ouyi's works included many subjects and were later compiled by his Dharma disciples, for a total of twenty books.

Brahma Net Sutra [Fanwang Jing]: T: vol. 24, no. 1484; translated into Chinese by Kumarajiva during the Latter Qin Dynasty. It describes the stages of cultivation in the bodhisattva path, the ten major precepts, and the forty-eight minors that should be upheld.

Buddhist Reference Books [Fo Guang Congshu]: Ten volumes in total; written by Master Hsing Yun; published in 1995 in Taiwan. This series is divided into ten categories: 1) Doctrines; 2) Scriptures; 3) the Buddha; 4) Disciples; 5) History; 6) Schools; 7) Ceremony and Rules; 8) Applications of Buddhism; 9) Literature and Writings; and 10) Humanistic Buddhism.

Chinese Buddhist Sutra Series [Zhong'guo Fojiao Jingdian Baozang]: One-hundred thirty-two volumes in total; published in 1998 in Taiwan by Fo Guang Shan.

Chronicle of Master Xuyun [Xuyun Heshang Nianpu]: Records the events of Master Xuyun's life, who was born in 1840 and died in 1959. He was a famous master of five Chan Schools (Caodong, Linji, Yunmen, Fayan, and Guiyang) in Chinese Buddhism.

Collection of Great Treasures [Maharatnakuta Sutra]: Ch. *Da Baoji Jing*. The title refers to the accumulation of great Dharma treasures and innumerable methods. Its major emphasis is related to the bodhisattvas' cultivation methods and the records that predicted their progress in attaining Buddhahood. The methods include the teachings and practices of emptiness, and the Pure Land and Esoteric schools.

Collective Sutra on Six Perfections [Liudu Ji Jing]: T: vol. 3, no. 152; translated into Chinese by Kang Senghui (?-280 C.E.) in the kingdom of Wu during the Three Kingdoms Period. It is a collection of ninety-one stories on Sakyamuni Buddha's fulfillment of the bodhisattva path in his past lives. The sutra's major doctrines focus on the six perfections–giving charity, upholding precepts, patience, diligence, meditative concentration, and prajna-wisdom.

Commentary on the Bei Sutra [Fo Shuo Bei Jing Chao]: T: vol. 17, no. 790; translated by Zhiqian during the Three Kingdoms Period; consists of one fascicle.

Commentary on the Main Mahayana Doctrines [Dosheng Baoyao Yi Lun]: T: vol. 32, no. 1635; translated by Fahu, Weijing, et al. It describes the Dharma methods of Mahayana practice and cultivation for Buddhists.

Commentary on the Stages of Yogacara Practitioners [Yogacarabhumi Sastra]: Ch. *Yuqie Shidi Lun*; T: vol. 30, no. 1579; discoursed by Maitreya Bodhisattva; recorded by Asanga and translated into Chinese by Xuanzang. This commentary is the basic text for the Yogacara School and the most important teaching in the Mind-Only School. It is also known as the *Commentary on the Seventeen Stages*.

Compendium of the Five Records of Chan Teachings [Wudeng Huiyuan]: *Svastika Corrected and Extended Tripitaka [Xu Zang Jing]*: vol. 138, p. 1-831; written by Puji of the Southern Song Dynasty; consists of twenty fascicles. It records the stories and historical events of the seven ancient Buddhas, the twenty-seven Indian patriarchs, and Chinese Chan masters.

Condensed Techniques of Stopping Delusion and Seeing Truth [*Xiao Zhi Guan*]: T: vol. 46, no. 1915; also known as *Xiuxi Zhiguan Zuochan Fayao,* discoursed by Zhiyi during the Sui Dynasty.

Connected Discourses of the Buddha [*Samyuktagama Sutra*]: Ch. *Za Ahan Jing*; in Pali, *Samyutta Nikaya.* It was translated into Chinese by Gunabhadra (394-468 C.E.) and contains 1,362 sutras in 50 fascicles (T: vol. 2, no. 99). It is named such because those whom the Buddha taught included bhiksus, bhiksunis, upaskas, upasikas, and heavenly beings; the teachings included several subjects such as the Four Noble Truths, Noble Eightfold Path, and dependent origination. There are now two English versions. One was translated by Bhikkhu Bodhi, and the other was translated by El Woodward, entitled *Kindred Sayings Vol. I-V.*

Dharma Garden of Buddhism [*Fayuan Zhulin*]: The work of Daoshi (?-683 C.E.), finished in 668 C.E. (T: vol. 53, no. 2122). It is a kind of Buddhist encyclopedia that describes Buddhist philosophy, terminology, and "fashu."

Diamond Sutra [*Vajracchedika Prajna Paramita Sutra*]: Ch. *Jingang Jing.* Translated into Chinese by Kumarajiva, Bodhiruci and Zhendi (T: vol. 8, no. 235, 236 & 237). "Vajracchedika" means "the diamond that cuts through afflictions, ignorance, delusions, or illusions." "Prajnaparamita" is "the perfection of wisdom," or "the understanding that brings sentient begins across the sea of suffering to the other shore."

Essential Points of Buddhism [*Shishi Yao Lan*]: T: vol. 54, no. 2127; compiled by Daocheng during the Song Dynasty (in 1019 C.E.). It describes basic Buddhist knowledge, teachings, and rules of monasteries.

Explanation of the Vimalakirti Sutra [*Jing Ming Jing Guanzhong Shi Chao*]: T: vol. 85, no. 2778; written by Daoyi during the Tang

Dynasty; consists of two fascicles.

Explanation on the Passages and Sentences of the Lotus Sutra [Miao Fa Lianhua Jing Wenju]: Also known as *Fahua Wenju*; T: vol. 34, no. 1718; discoursed by Zhiyi at Guangzhai Temple in 587 (Sui Dynasty); twenty fascicles in total. One of the three great Fahua works, all three written by Zhiyi.

Father and Son Sutra [Fuzi Heji Jing]: T: vol. 11, no. 320; translated by Richeng of the Song Dynasty; consists of twenty fascicles.

Five Part Vinaya [Mahisasaka Vinaya]: Ch. *Wu Fen Lu*; T: vol. 22, no. 1421; the precepts of the Mahisasaka School. The original Sanskrit version was acquired by Faxian Sanzang from Sri Lanka and translated into Chinese by Buddhajiva and Zhu Daosheng. It includes 251 precepts for the bhiksus and 370 precepts for the bhiksunis.

Flower Ornament Sutra [Avatamsaka Sutra]: Ch. *Huayan Jing*. The complete Sanskrit title is *Buddhavatamsaka Mahavaipulya Sutra*; in English, the *Flower Ornament Scripture* or the *Flower Garland Sutra*. It is one of the most important sutras of Mahayana Buddhism. The major teachings in the Huayan School are based on this sutra. In the *Chinese Buddhist Canon*, there are three versions: 1) Sixty Fascicles, translated by Buddhabhadra (359-429 C.E.); 2) Eighty Fascicles, translated by Siksananda (652-710 C.E.); and 3) Forty Fascicles, translated by Prajna (734-? C.E.) (T: no. 278, no. 279, and no. 293). An English translation was completed by Thomas Cleary and published by Shambhala Publications in 1993.

Fo Guang Buddhist Encyclopedia [Fo Guang Da Cidian]: One index and seven volumes in total; published in 1988 in Taiwan by Fo Guang Publications.

Fo Guang Buddhist Textbooks [Fo Guang Jiaoke Shu]: Twelve volumes in total; each volume consists of twenty chapters; published in 1999 in Taiwan by Fo Guang Shan.

Four Part Vinaya [Dharmagupta Vinaya]: Ch. *Si Fen Lu*. Originally, it was the Vinaya of the Dharmagupta School in the Theravada System (known as "Arya-sthavira-nikaya" in Sanskrit). It was translated into Chinese by Zhu Fonian and Buddhayasas in 410-412 C.E. (T: vol. 30, no. 1564).

Gradual Discourses of the Buddha [Ekottarikagama Sutra]: Ch. *Zeng Yi Ahan Jing*; in Pali, *Anguttara Nikaya*. Translated into Chinese by Qutan Sengqie Tipo (Skt. Gautama Sangha Deva?) It contains 52 fascicles and 472 sutras. Compared with other agamas, it is the most recent and embraces the Mahayana philosophy. It was named such because the Buddha gradually discourses upon seven methods of practice.

Great Compilation of Monastic Rules [Mahasanghavinaya]: Ch. *Mohe Sengqi Lu*. Translated by Buddhabhadra and Faxian (T: vol. 22, no. 1425), it is a collection of monastic rules transmitted in the Mahasanghika School, and describes in detail the precepts for the bhiksus and bhiksunis: 218 precepts for bhiksus and 277 precepts for bhiksunis.

Great Nirvana Sutra [Parinirvana Sutra]: Ch. *Bo Nihuan Jing*; T: vol. 1, no. 6; different from the translated version of the *Mahaparinirvana Sutra*. The translator is unknown. It offers that the Dharma-body always abides, all sentient beings possess the Buddha Nature, and the "icchantika" can also attain Buddhahood.

Great Techniques of Stopping Delusion and Seeing Truth [Mohe Zhiguan]: T. vol. 46, no. 1911. This work was instructed by Master Zhiyi and recorded by his disciple, Guanding, in 594 C.E. The content describes the meditation methods of Zhi (stopping) and Guan (seeing), as well as Master Zhiyi's personal meditation experiences.

Historical Records of the Dharma Gem [Lidai Fabao Ji]: T: vol. 49, no. 2034; written by Fei Changfang during the Sui Dynasty. It is one of the records on the propagation of the Dharma from the time when Buddhism was transmitted into China until the period of the Sui Dynasty. It is also a catalog of numerous translated sutras and Buddhist works.

History of the Buddhist Patriarchs [Fozu Lidai Tongzai]: T: vol. 49, no.

2036; consists of twenty-two fascicles in total, written by Nianchang during the Yuan Dynasty. It records the history of Buddhism and describes important Buddhist affairs and events from the period of the seven ancient Buddhas to the year 1333 C.E.

Imperially Reviewed Encyclopedia of the Taiping Era [*Taiping Yulan*]: One thousand fascicles in total; written and completed by Li Fang, et al., in 977 C.E. (the second year of the Taiping Xing'guo Period during the reign of Emperor Taizong of the Song Dynasty). It contains various subjects, similar to other encyclopedias of that time.

Important Selections from the Sutras [*Zhu Jing Yao Ji*]: T: vol. 54, no. 2123; twenty fascicles in total; also known as the *Treatise on the Retribution of Wholesomeness and Unwholesomeness*, written by Daoshi in 659 C.E. (Tang Dynasty). It is similar to a Buddhist encyclopedia. A later work–*Dharma Garden of Buddhism* [*Fayuan Zhulin*]–is an extended version of this book.

Jataka Sutras: One of the twelve sections of the *Chinese Buddhist Canon*, recording the stories and events of Sakyamuni Buddha's previous lives when he fulfilled the bodhisattva path.

Jingde Records of the Transmission of the Lamp [*Jingde Chuan Deng Lu*]: T: vol. 51, no. 2076; written by Daoyuan during the Song Dynasty; one of the historical books of the Chinese Chan School. It records the Dharma legacy since the seven ancient Buddhas, which includes a total of fifty-two generations and 1,701 figures.

Lankavatara Sutra [*Leng Qie Jing*]: T: vol. 16, no. 670; translated by Gunabhadra in 443; a total of four fascicles. It is a representation of Mahayana sutras during the latter period of the Indian Buddhism. Its premise is that the existence of all phenomena is the result of the mind and its activities. It also emphasizes that the root of delusions originates from habitual tendencies, and not awakening to all dharmas is the result of one's mind.

Long Discourses of the Buddha [*Dirghagama Sutra*]: Ch. *Chang Ahan Jing*; in Pali, *Digha Nikaya*. Translated into Chinese by Buddhayasas and Zhu Fonian in 413 C.E. (T: vol. 1, no. 1). This version is composed of thirty sutras in four parts. The Pali version includes thirty-four sutras in three parts. The content varies slightly between the two versions due to interpretations and translations that sought to emphasize different schools of Buddhism.

Longshu Extended Composition of Pure Land [*Longshu Zeng'guang Jingtu Wen*]: T: vol. 47, no. 1970; written by Wang Rixiu in 1160. It is a collection of sutras, commentaries, and biographies relating to rebirth in the Western Pure Land.

Middle Length Discourses of the Buddha [*Madhyamagama Sutra*]: Ch. *Zhong Ahan Jing*; T: vol. 1, no. 26; translated into Chinese by Samghadeva; in Pali, *Majjhima Nikaya*. It is named *The Middle Length Discourses* because each chapter is neither too long nor too short; in other words, it is a collection of the sutras that are neither long nor short. The contents include the words and deeds of Sakyamuni Buddha and his disciples and the basic doctrines of Buddhism, such as the Four Noble Truths and the Twelve Links of Dependent Origination.

Monastic Regulations of Baizhang Revised by the Emperor Shun of Yuan Dynasty [*Chixiu Baizhang Qing'gui*]: T: vol. 48; no. 2025; written by Baizhang Huaihai; two fascicles in total. Due to the lack of systematic regulations and rules as well as an absence of Chan monasteries in the beginning of the Chinese Chan School, Chan Master Baizhang founded a system of regulations for Chan monasteries that describes and records in detail the rules of life in a Chan monastery.

Moon Lamp Samadhi Sutra [*Samadhirajachadrapradipa Sutra*]: Ch. *Yue Deng Sanmei Jing*; T: vol. 15, no. 639; translated into Chinese by Narendrayasas (490-589 C.E.) This sutra describes the Buddha discoursing upon the teachings to Candraprabha (the Moon Light Bodhisattva). The teachings are on how to achieve the five perfections of giving, upholding precepts, patience, and diligence through the mind of equality, protecting others, and no "poisons."

Nirvana Sutra: Skt. *Mahaparinirvana Sutra*. There are three versions in the *Chinese Buddhist Canon*. One version was translated by Faxian, called *Fo Shuo Dabo Nihuan Jing*, with six fascicles (T: vol. 12, no. 376). Another was translated by Dharmaraksa, named *Dabo Niepan Jing,* with forty fascicles (T: vol. 12, no. 374). A third is also named such, but with additional content and revision by Master Huiyan of the Song Dynasty. The latter version consists of thirty-six fascicles (T: vol. 12, no. 375).

Path of Purification [Visuddhimagga]: *Pali Tripitaka*: vol. 62-64; written by Buddhaghosa during the 5th century; translated into English by Bhikkhu Nanamoli. This book is an important commentary on the teachings of the Theravada School.

Precious Teachings of the Chan Masters [Chanlin Baoxun]: T: vol. 48, no. 2022; translated into Chinese by Jingshan during the Song Dynasty. It records the sayings of more than three hundred Chan Masters of the Song Dynasty.

Record of Buddhist Schools in India and Southern Asia [Nanhai Jigui Neifa Zhuan]: Or known as *A Record of the Buddhist Religions as Practiced in India and the Malay Archipelago* (T: vol. 54, no. 2125); written by Yijing; four fascicles. It is an important source for the study of 7th century Buddhist orders, sanghas, and Vinaya in India and Southern Asia.

Record of Monastics' Virtuous Deeds [Zimen Chongxing Lu]: *The Svastika Corrected and Extended Tripitaka*: vol. 148, p.799-832; one fascicle only; written by Zhuhong (1532-1612 C.E.) during the Ming Dynasty. It contains brief descriptions of the virtuous deeds of one hundred monastics from the time of the Buddha to the Ming Dynasty.

Record of the Mirror of the Mind [Zongjing Lu]: T: vol. 48, no. 2016; written by Yongming Yanshou in 961 C.E.; one hundred fascicles in total. It broadly collects and quotes from sixty sutras and commentaries, as well as from the writings of three hundred Chinese sages and saints.

Records of Monastics at Tianmu Mountain [Xi Tianmu Zushan Zhi]: Written by Guangbin during the Ming Dynasty and later revised and updated by Jijie during the Qing Dynasty; contains twelve fascicles in total.

Repentance Text of the Mahisasaka School [*Mishase Jiemo Ben*]: T: vol. 22, no. 1424; recorded and collected by Aitong of the Tang Dynasty, it includes ten sections.

Ritual of the Triple Gem Refuge and Five Precepts Ceremony: Ch. *Sanqui Wujie Zheng Fan*. The work of the Vinaya by Master Jianyue.

Subcommentary on the Flower Ornament Sutra [*Huayan Jing Sui Shu Yanyi Chao*]: T: vol. 36, no. 1736; ninety fascicles in total; written by Cheng'guan during the Tang Dynasty. It is an explanation of the *Commentary on the Flower Ornament Sutra* [*Huayan Jing Shu*].

Surata Sutra Discoursed by the Buddha [*Suratapariccha Sutra*]: Ch. *Fo Shuo Xulai Jing*; T: vol. 12, no. 329; translated into Chinese by Bai Yan in Cao Wei of the Three Kingdoms Period. This sutra describes the story of a poor man named Surata who lived in Sravasti. Surata was a man of great virtue who upheld the precepts and cultivated the ten wholesome conducts. Even when Sakra Deva tried to threaten him with force and lure him with gold and precious gems, Surata was not distracted from his determination to seek liberation for himself and all sentient beings. The rest of the sutra describes the argument between King Prasenajit and Surata on poverty and wealth. Finally, the Buddha taught them that the mind of purity is like richness, while the mind greed is like poverty. After that, King Prasenajit took refuge in the Buddha.

Sutra Requested by Visesacinta Brahma Deva [*Visesacinta-brahma-pariprccha Sutra*]: Ch. *Siyi Fantian Suo Wen Jing*; T: vol. 15, no. 586; translated into Chinese by Kumarajiva during the Yao Qin Dynasty; contains a total of four fascicles. It documents the Buddha discoursing to Visesacinta Brahma Deva and Jaliniprabha Bodhisattva that the true nature of all dharmas is emptiness.

Sutra Discoursed by the Inconceivable Light Bodhisattva [*Busiyiguang Pusa Suo Shuo Jing*]: T: vol. 14, no. 484; translated into Chinese by Kumarajiva in the Latter Qin Dynasty; one fascicle.

Sutra of All Wisdom and Virtues [*Yiqie Zhi De Jing*]: Or Ch. *Jianbei Yiqie Zhi De Jing*; T: vol. 10, no. 285; translated into Chinese by Dharmaraksa during the Western Jin Dynasty; five fascicles in total. Its content describes the Dharma methods of cultivation on the ten stages of the bodhisattva path.

Sutra of Bodhisattva Stages [*Bodhisattvabhumi Sutra*]: Ch. *Pusa Dichi Jing;* T: vol. 30, no. 1581; translated into Chinese by Dharmaraksa during the Bei Liang Dynasty; ten fascicles in total. Although named a "sutra," its contents are more similar to a commentary. It describes the skillful means of Mahayana bodhisattvas' practice, categorized into three parts: the beginning, the intermediate, and the ultimate. It also includes the Mahayana precepts.

Sutra of the Buddha's Diagnosis [*Fo Yi Jing*]: T: vol. 17, no. 793; translated into Chinese by Zhu Luyan and Zhiyue during the Wu Dynasty in the Three Kingdoms Period; contains one fascicle.

Sutra of Buddha's Discourse on the Four Matters Requested by Ananda [*Fo Shuo Anan Si Shi Jing*]: T: vol. 14, no. 493; translated into Chinese by Zhiqian of the Wu Dynasty during the Three Kingdoms Period; contains one fascicle.

Sutra of Buddha's Discourse to King Prasenajit [*Rulai Shijiao Shengjun Wang Jing*]: T: vol. 14, no. 515; translated into Chinese by Xuanzang; documenting the education of King Prasenajit by the Buddha while in the city of Sravasti on the ways of ruling a nation, the concept of impermanence, and the importance of ending afflictions.

Sutra of Contemplation on the Practicing Methods of Samantabhadra Bodhisattva [*Guan Puxian Pusa Xingfa Jing*]: T: vol. 9, no. 277; translated into Chinese by Dharmamitra during the Liu Song Dynasty. The impending parinirvana of the Buddha prompted him to discourse this sutra while at Mahavana. Prior to this sutra, the Buddha had also discoursed on the *Lotus Sutra*. When the Buddha declared that he would be entering parinirvana, Ananda pleaded with the Buddha to instruct the Sangha on the practice of the Mahayana dharma methods and its doctrines. That led to the Buddha teaching the methods of practicing

Samantabhadra, the method of repenting unwholesome deeds, and the virtues of repentance.

Sutra of the Filial Child Discoursed by the Buddha [*Fo Shuo Xiaozi Jing*]: T: vol. 16, no. 687; only one fascicle. The translator is unknown. In the sutra, the Buddha instructs that the true way of filial piety is to make oneself and one's parents take refuge in the Triple Gem and uphold the five precepts.

Sutra of Golden Light [*Suvarnaprabhasttama Sutra*]: Ch. *Jin Guangming Zui Sheng Wang Jing*; translated into Chinese by Yijing (T: vol. 16, no. 665). One of three sutras for protecting the nation (the other two are the *Lotus Sutra* and *Karunikaraja Prajnaparamita Sutra*). This sutra describes the virtues and merits of performing the Golden Light Repentance, as well as the belief of being protected by the Four Great Kings and the benefits of this kind of belief.

Sutra of Illuminating Light [*Chu Yao Jing*]: T: vol. 4, no. 212; contains a total of thirty fascicles; written by Dharmatrata; translated into Chinese by Zhu Fonian during the Yao Qin Dynasty. This sutra elaborates on the concepts of impermanence, cultivation through upholding precepts, practicing concentration, and accumulating wisdom that leads to liberation; all of which are expressed through parables.

Sutra of Loyalty [*Zhong Xin Jing*]: Or the *Sutra of Loyalty Discoursed by the Buddha* [*Fo Shuo Xhong Xin Jing*]; T: vol. 17, no. 743; translated into Chinese by Tan Wulan (Dharmaraksa?). This sutra is about the Buddha teaching five bhiksus that true loyalty is to learn and know the five aggregates, the twelve links of dependent origination, and the four applications of mindfulness.

Sutra of Miscellaneous Treasures [*Samyuktaratnapitaka Sutra*]: Ch. *Za Baozang Jing*; T: vol. 4, no. 203; translated into Chinese by Kinkara and Tanyao; ten fascicles in total. It is a collection of stories on the Buddha and his disciples as well as important events that occurred following the Buddha's parinirvana.

Sutra of the Buddha of Infinite Life [*Sukhavativyuha Sutra*]: Or known as *Larger Sutra on Amitayus* and Ch. *Wu Liang Shou Jing*; T: vol. 12, no.

360; translated into Chinese by Samaghavarman. It is one of three basic texts of the Pure Land School. The other two are the *Sutra on Contemplation of the Buddha of Infinite Life* (or the *Sutra on Contemplation of Amitayus*) and the *Amitabha Sutra* (or the *Smaller Sutra on Amitayus*).

Sutra of the Great Wisdom [*Mahaprajnaparamita Sutra*]: Or known as the *Sutra on the Perfection of Great Wisdom*; T: vol. 5-vol. 7; six hundred fascicles in total; translated into Chinese by Xuanzang during the Tang Dynasty.

Sutra of the Great-Teacher King [*Da Jiao Wang Jing*]: T: vol. 18, no. 865; translated into Chinese by Amoghavajra; three fascicles in total.

Sutra of the King Fanmonan [*Fanmonan Guowang Jing*]: T: vol. 14, no. 521; one fascicle only; translated into Chinese during the Western Jin Dynasty.

Sutra of the Past Vows of the Earth Store Bodhisattva [*Kstigarbhapranidhana Sutra*]: Ch. *Dizang Pusa Ben Yuan Jing*; T: vol. 13, no. 412; translated into Chinese by Siksananda; two fascicles comprising thirteen chapters. It describes the merits and virtues of the Earth Store (Ksitigarbha) Bodhisattva's past vows. It also states that the recitation of this sutra can eliminate unwholesome karmas.

Sutra of the Teachings Bequeathed by the Buddha: Ch. *Fo Yijiao Jing*; T: vol. 12, no. 389; translated into Chinese by Kumarajiva. This sutra describes the Buddha's last teachings before he entered parinirvana. These teachings instruct the disciples to follow the "pratimoksa," see it as the teacher, and rely on it for guiding the five sense organs and attaining freedom.

Sutra of the Ten Great Dharma Wheels [*Dasacakraksitigarbha Sutra*]: Ch. *Da Fang Guang Shilun Jing*; T: vol. 13, no. 410; eight fascicles in total. Translator is unknown. It describes the merits and virtues of Ksitigarbha Bodhisattva, and ways of turning unwholesome karmas to wholesome karmas.

Sutra of Wisdom and Foolishness [Damamuka-nidana Sutra]: Ch. *Xianyu Jing*; T: vol. 4, no. 202; also known as the *Sutra on the Causes and Conditions of Wisdom and Foolishness*; translated into Chinese by Huijue during the Yuan Wei Dynasty. It contains various parables about the wise and fools.

Sutra on the Buddha's Ascension to the Trayastrimsas Heaven to Discourse the Dharma to His Mother [Fo Sheng Daolitian Wei Mo Shuo Fa]: T: vol. 12, no. 383; also known as the *Mahamaya Sutra*; translated into Chinese by Tanjing during the Northern Qi Dynasty; two fascicles in total. The first part of the sutra describes how the Buddha ascends to the Trayastrimsas Heaven and discourses the Dharma to his mother, Mahamaya, and after hearing the Dharma, Mahamaya attains the first fruit of arhatship. The second part describes when the Buddha enters parinirvana, Mahamaya descends from Heaven to see the Buddha.

Sutra on the Contemplation of the Buddha of Infinite Life [Amitayurdhyana Sutra]: Or known as *Sutra on Contemplation of Amitayus*, or *Sutra of Sixteen Contemplations*; Ch. *Guan Wuliangshou Jing*; T: vol. 12, no. 365; translated into Chinese by Kalayasas during the Liu Song Dynasty; one fascicle only. It describes sixteen methods of contemplating on the Western Pure Land. It is one of three sutras of the Pure Land School.

Sutra on the Contemplation of the Mind [Xindi Guan Jing]: Or Ch. *Dasheng Bensheng Xindi Guan Jing*; T: vol. 3, no. 159; translated into Chinese by Prajna (734-?); eight fascicles in total. It describes the Buddha's discourse at Vulture Peak to Manjusri, Maitreya, and other great bodhisattvas on the contemplation of the mind, the elimination of delusions, and the attainment of the path of Buddhahood.

Sutra on the Ascent of Maitreya [Mi'le Shangsheng Jing]: T: vol. 14, no. 452; translated into Chinese by Juqu Liangsheng in the Liu Song Dynasty; one of Maitreya's three sutras. Among those sutras, this was the last to be developed and completed.

Sutra on the Collection of Important Points on All Dharmas [Zhu Fa

Jiyao Jing]: T: vol. 17, no. 728; translated into Chinese by Richeng during the Song Dynasty; ten fascicles in total.

Sutra on the Descent of Maitreya [Mi'le Xiasheng Jing]: T: vol. 14, no. 453; translated into Chinese by Dharmaraksa during the Western Jin Dynasty; one of Maitreya's three sutras. It describes Maitreya Bodhisattva's descent from heaven to this world, his cultivation, and his attainment of Buddhahood and his Pure Land.

Sutra on the Difficulty of Repaying the Kindness of Parents [Fo Shuo Fumu En Zhong Nan Bao Jing]: T: vol. 16, no. 684; translated into Chinese by An Shigao; only one fascicle. The sutra documents that the best ways to repay the kindness of one's parents are to lead them to believe in the Triple Gem, uphold the precepts, hear and learn the Dharma, give charity, and gain wisdom.

Sutra on the Distinguishing Merits and Virtues [Punya Vibhanga Sutra]: Ch. *Fo Shuo Fenbie Gongde Jing*; translated into Chinese during the Eastern Han Dynasty.

Sutra on the Eight Purification Precepts [Astangasamanvagata Sutra]: Ch. *Fo Shuo Baguanzhai Jing*; T: vol. 1, no. 89; translated into Chinese by Juqu Liangsheng during the Liu Song Dynasty; contains one fascicle. In this sutra, the Buddha discourses to Visakha on the eight purification precepts and the merits of upholding precepts.

Sutra on the Four Unattainables Discoursed by the Buddha [Fo Shuo Si Bukede Jing]: T: vol. 17, no. 770; translated into Chinese by Dharmaraksa from 266 to 313 in the Western Jin Dynasty; contains one fascicle. In this sutra, the Buddha discourses that to be forever young, without sickness, without aging, and immortality are four unattainable things.

Sutra on the Mindfulness and Purification of the Mind [Fajue Jingxin Jing]: T: vol. 12, no. 327; translated into Chinese by Jnanagupta, and includes a total of two fascicles.

Sutra on the Nirvana of King Suddhodana Discoursed by the Buddha [Fo Shuo Jingfan Wang Boniepan Jing]: T: vol. 14, no. 512; translated into

Chinese by Juqu Liangsheng (?-464) during the Liu Song Dynasty; only one fascicle. This sutra describes the attendance of the Buddha, Ananda, and others at King Suddhodana's funeral, with the purpose of emphasizing filial piety, and to instruct the teachings of impermanence, suffering, emptiness, and non-self.

Sutra on the Prajna-Paramita for the Benevolent King [*Renwang Huguo Bore Boluomiduo Jing*]: T: vol. 8, no. 246; translated into Chinese by Amoghavajra (705-774) in 765 C.E.; two fascicles in total. This is a later translation based on an earlier translation by Kumarajiva. It is one of the three sutras for protecting the nation (the other two are the *Lotus Sutra* and the *Sutra of Golden Light*).

Sutra on the Principles of Six Paramitas [*Liu Boluomiduo Jing*]: Or Ch. *Dasheng Liqu Liu Boluomiduo Jing*, or *Liu Du Jing*; T: vol. 8, no. 261; translated into Chinese by Prajna, also named Bore Sanzang, in 788 C.E. This sutra describes how to protect the nation and how to practice the six perfections of the bodhisattva's cultivation. The ten chapters are: 1) taking refuge in the Triple Gem, 2) mantra for protecting the nation, 3) awakening the enlightened mind, 4) non-regression, 5) the perfection of giving charity, 6) the perfection of upholding the precepts, 7) the perfection of patience, 8) the perfection of diligence, 9) the perfection of meditation, and 10) the perfection of prajna-wisdom.

Sutra on the Prophecy of Mahasatya's Enlightenment [*Bodhisattva Gocaropaya Visaya Vikurvananirdesa Sutra*]: Ch. *Dasazhe Niqianzi Suo Shuo Jing*; T: vol. 9, no. 272; translated into Chinese by Bodhiruci during the Yuan Wei Dynasty. This sutra is a documentation of Mahasatya's instruction on the Mahayana doctrines in response to Manjusri's questions. Following Mahasatya's instruction, the Buddha praised his instruction and cultivation, and the Buddha then prophesied Mahasatya's enlightenment.

Sutra on the Treasury of Truth [*Dharmapada Sutra*]: Ch. *Faju Jing*. Also known as *The Word of Truth, The Treasury of Truth*, or *The Treasures of the Truth*. The Chinese translation (T: vol. 4, no. 210) has two fascicles and a total of thirty-nine chapters, including seven-hundred-and-fifty-two verses.

Sutra on the Treasury of Truth with Parables [*Dharmapadavadana Sutra*]: Ch. *Faju Piyu Jing*; T: vol. 4, no. 211; translated into Chinese by Faju and Fali during the Western Jin Dynasty; has a total of 4 fascicles. It contains 230 verses from the *Sutra on the Treasury of Truth*, plus the parable stories.

Sutra on Upasaka Precepts [*Upasakasila Sutra*]: Ch. *Youpose Jie Jing*; translated into Chinese by Dharmaraksa (385-433) in 426 C.E. (T: vol. 24, no. 1488). This sutra discusses taking refuge in the Triple Gem and the five precepts. It explains the bodhisattvas' right intention, making vows, practicing and learning, upholding precepts, diligence, meditation, and wisdom.

Syamaka Sutra: Ch. *Shanzi Jing*; T: vol. 3, no. 175; translated into Chinese by Shanjian during the Yao Qin Dynasty; has one fascicle only. In one of his previous lives, Sakyamuni Buddha was Syamaka. This sutra describes Syamaka's story and his cultivation on the bodhisattva path.

Ten Recitations Vinaya [*Sarvastivadin Vinaya*]: Ch. *Shi Song Lu*; T: vol. 23, no. 1435; translated into Chinese by Kumarajiva and Punyatara during the Yao Qin Dynasty; includes sixty-one fascicles in total. This *Vinaya* divides precepts into ten parts, and belongs to the Sarvastivada School in the Period of Sectarian Buddhism.

Treatise on the Perfection of Great Wisdom [*Mahaprajnaparamita Sastra*]: Ch. *Da Zhidu Lun*; the commentary of the *Mahaprajnaparamita Sutra*; T: vol. 25, no. 1509; written by Nagarjuna, the founder of the Madhyamika School, between the second and third century; translated into Chinese by Kumarajiva in 402-405 C.E. Kumarajiva was one of the four great translators in Chinese Buddhist history. This commentary includes detailed interpretations of Buddhist doctrines, philosophies, illustrations, legends, history, geography, rules of practice, as well as the definition and function of the sangha. Its main emphases are on the philosophy and spirit of the bodhisattva path in Mahayana Buddhism, and the practices of the six perfections.

Treatise on the Demonstration of Mind-Only [*Vidyamatrasiddhi Sastra*]: Also known as the *Demonstration of Consciousness-Only* (BDK Publications). Ch. *Cheng Weishi Lun.* It is the explanation of Vasubhandu's *Thirty Verses on Mind-Only.* This work was done by Dharmapala and nine other great commentators in 557 C.E.; then it was translated into Chinese by Xuanzang (T: vol. 31, no. 1585).

Treatise on the Middle Way [*Mulamadhyamaka Karika*]: T: vol. 30, no. 1564; Ch. *Zhong Guan Lun* or *Zhong Lun*; written by Nagarjuna, explained by Pingala, and translated into Chinese by Kumarajiva.

Ullumbana Sutra [*Yupanlan Jing*]: T: vol. 16, no. 685; translated into Chinese by Dharmaraksa. This sutra describes Maudgalyayana, who after witnessing his mother's fall and suffering in the realm of hungry ghosts, requests the Buddha to instruct the Dharma to liberate his mother. As a result, the Buddha instructed Maudgalyayana to make offerings of dishes and fruits to the Buddhas and sanghas of the ten directions, so that sentient beings in the realm of hungry ghosts can be liberated. This offering ceremony has since pervaded Chinese society and become a symbol of filial piety.

Vigilance for All Monastics [*Zimen Jingxun*]: T: vol. 48, no. 2023. The original edition was authored by Zexian during the Song Dynasty and later revised and re-compiled by Linji Monk Yongzhong in the Yuan Dynasty; a third revision was completed by Rujin. It includes over 170 key phrases of the virtuous monastics.

Vimalakirti Sutra [*Vimalakirtinirdesa Sutra*]: The main purposes of this sutra are to clarify the methods of practice for liberation that Vimalakirti achieved and to explain the practices of Mahayana bodhisattvas and the virtues that the layperson should fulfill.

Vinaya: Usually implying the basket of precepts, one of the *Tripitaka.* Specifically, it refers to *Pinaiye Lu* (T: vol. 24, no. 1464), which includes ten fascicles translated into Chinese by Zhu Fonian.